PETER'S

TOEFL*

GRAMMAR

FLASH

**The Quick Way to
Build Grammar Power**

Milada Broukal

* TOEFL® AND TWE® ARE REGISTERED TRADEMARKS OF EDUCATIONAL TESTING SERVICE, WHICH
WAS NOT INVOLVED IN THE PRODUCTION OF, AND DOES NOT ENDORSE, THIS PRODUCT.

About Peterson's

Founded in 1966, Peterson's, a division of Thomson Learning, is the nation's largest and most respected provider of lifelong learning online resources, software, reference guides, and books. The Education Supersite℠ at petersons.com—the Web's most heavily traveled education resource—has searchable databases and interactive tools for contacting U.S.-accredited institutions and programs. CollegeQuest℠ (CollegeQuest.com) offers a complete solution for every step of the college decision-making process. GradAdvantage™ (GradAdvantage.org), developed with Educational Testing Service, is the only electronic admissions service capable of sending official graduate test score reports with a candidate's online application. Peterson's serves over 55 million education consumers annually.

Thomson Learning is among the world's largest providers of lifelong learning information. Headquartered in Stamford, CT, with multiple offices worldwide, Thomson Learning is a division of The Thomson Corporation (TTC), one of the world's leading information companies. TTC operates mainly in the U.S., Canada, and the UK and has annual revenues of over US$6 billion. The Corporation's common shares are traded on the Toronto, Montreal, and London stock exchanges. For more information, visit TTC's Internet address at www.thomcorp.com.

TOEFL® and TWE® are registered trademarks of Educational Testing Service.

Visit Peterson's Education Center on the Internet (World Wide Web) at
www.petersons.com

Copyright © 1997 by Peterson's

All rights reserved. No part of this work may be reproduced, transcribed, or used in any form or by any means—graphic, electronic, or mechanical, including photocopying, recording, taping, Web distribution, or information storage and retrieval systems—without the prior written permission of the publisher.

For permission to use material from this text or product, contact us by

- Web: www.thomsonrights.com
- Phone: 1-800-730-2214
- Fax: 1-800-730-2215

TOEFL® GRAMMAR Flash was adapted from *TOEFL® Test Assistant: Grammar* by Milada Broukal and published by Heinle & Heinle/ITP.

Library of Congress Cataloging-in-Publication Data

Broukal, Milada.
    TOEFL grammar flash : the quick way to build grammar power / Milada Broukal.
       p.   cm.
    ISBN 0-7689-0509-5
    1. English language—Textbooks for foreign speakers. 2. English language—Grammar—Examinations—Study guides. 3. Test of English as a foreign language—Study guides. 4. English language—Examinations—Study guides. I. Title.
PE1128.B71473   1997
428.2'4'076—dc21   97-34268
                                                                                         CIP

Printed in Canada

10 9 8 7 6 5 4 3 2

CONTENTS

Acknowledgments	vii
To the Teacher	ix
To the Student	xi
The Structure and Written Expression Section of the TOEFL® Test	xiii

PART 1: TYPES OF STRUCTURE AND WRITTEN EXPRESSION QUESTIONS — 1

CHAPTER 1: NOUNS — 2
- Introduction: The Brain — 2
- Grammar: Singular and Plural Nouns — 4
- On the TOEFL® Test — 8
- Exercises on Nouns — 9

CHAPTER 2: PRONOUNS — 11
- Introduction: Penguins — 11
- Grammar: Pronouns — 13
- On the TOEFL® Test — 19
- Exercises on Pronouns — 21

CHAPTER 3 PARTS OF A SENTENCE — 23
- Introduction: Phyllis Wheatley — 23
- Grammar: Parts of a Sentence — 24
- On the TOEFL® Test — 30
- Exercises on Parts of a Sentence — 31

CHAPTER 4: VERBS — 33
- Introduction: The Olympics — 33
- Grammar: Verbs — 35
- On the TOEFL® Test — 44
- Exercises on Verbs — 46

CHAPTER 5: PREPOSITIONS — 48
    Introduction: Mount St. Helens — 48
    Grammar: Prepositions — 49
    On the TOEFL® Test — 55
    Exercises on Prepositions — 56

CHAPTER 6: ARTICLES — 58
    Introduction: Islands — 58
    Grammar: Articles — 60
    On the TOEFL® Test — 65
    Exercises on Articles — 66

CHAPTER 7: NOUN CLAUSES — 68
    Introduction: Michael Faraday — 68
    Grammar: Noun Clauses — 69
    On the TOEFL® Test — 73
    Exercises on Noun Clauses — 74

CHAPTER 8: ADJECTIVE CLAUSES — 76
    Introduction: American Indian Smoke Signals — 76
    Grammar: Adjective Clauses — 77
    On the TOEFL® Test — 82
    Exercises on Adjective Clauses — 83

CHAPTER 9: ADVERB CLAUSES — 85
    Introduction: Distant Galaxies — 85
    Grammar: Adverb Clauses — 86
    On the TOEFL® Test — 91
    Exercises on Adverb Clauses — 92

CHAPTER 10: PREPOSITIONAL PHRASES — 94
    Introduction: Land Art — 94
    Grammar: Prepositional Phrases — 95
    On the TOEFL® Test — 98
    Exercises on Prepositional Phrases — 99

CHAPTER 11: COMPARATIVES AND SUPERLATIVES — 102
    Introduction: Violins — 102
    Grammar: Comparatives and Superlatives — 103
    On the TOEFL® Test — 107
    Exercises on Comparatives and Superlatives — 108

CHAPTER 12: CONJUNCTIONS — 110
- Introduction: The Soya Bean's Industrial Uses — 110
- Grammar: Conjunctions — 111
- On the TOEFL® Test — 115
- Exercises on Conjunctions — 116

CHAPTER 13: PARALLEL STRUCTURE — 118
- Introduction: Vitamin C — 118
- Grammar: Parallel Structure — 119
- On the TOEFL® Test — 122
- Exercises on Parallel Structure — 123

CHAPTER 14: WORD ORDER — 125
- Introduction: Computers — 125
- Grammar: Word Order — 127
- On the TOEFL® Test — 130
- Exercises on Inversion — 131

CHAPTER 15: WORD FORMS — 133
- Introduction: Benjamin Franklin — 133
- Grammar: Word Forms — 134
- On the TOEFL® Test — 139
- Exercises on Word Forms — 140

CHAPTER 16: WORD CHOICE AND REDUNDANCY — 142
- Introduction: Asbestos — 142
- Grammar: Word Choice — 144
- Redundancy — 149
- On the TOEFL® Test — 150
- Exercises on Word Choice and Redundancy — 151

PART II: STRUCTURE AND WRITTEN EXPRESSION PRACTICE TESTS — 153
PRACTICE TEST 1 — 154
PRACTICE TEST 2 — 160
PRACTICE TEST 3 — 166
PRACTICE TEST 4 — 172
PRACTICE TEST 5 — 178

Answer Key — 185

ACKNOWLEDGMENTS

I would like to thank the following professionals for their contribution by reviewing *TOEFL® Grammar Flash* and giving many helpful insights and suggestions:

Paul Abraham, Simmons College
Lida Baker, University of California, Los Angeles
Kelly Franklin, Maryville College
Tom Leverett, Southern Illinois University at Carbondale
Virginia Martin, Bowling Green State University
Nancy Pfingstag, University of North Carolina at Charlotte
Bruce Rogers, Economics Institute

TO THE TEACHER

TOEFL® Grammar Flash prepares students for Section 2, Structure and Written Expression, of the TOEFL® Test. The text is designed for both self-study and classroom use.

The book is divided into Parts I and II. Part I includes sixteen chapters, each focusing on a grammar area tested in the Structure and Written Expression section of the test. Part II provides five Structure and Written Expression practice tests.

In Part I, the chapters are organized in order of difficulty, and not according to the frequency of errors that occur on the test. However, if time is limited, the five chapters indicated below, which treat grammatical issues that most often cause errors on the TOEFL® Test, can be studied first. The remaining chapters have about the same ratio of error frequency and can be studied in any order.

Chapter 15	Word Forms
Chapter 16	Word Choice and Redundancy
Chapter 4	Verbs
Chapter 13	Parallel Structure
Chapter 2	Pronouns

In each chapter the errors made in both the Structure part and the Written Expression part of the TOEFL® Test are covered together. The "On the TOEFL® Test" section of each chapter gives examples of errors tested in the Structure part or the Written Expression part as they occur on the test. Also, the grammar focus exercise that follows is based on errors made in the Structure and Written Expression section.

Each chapter in Part I opens with a reading passage of general interest. The aim of this passage is to provide a context for the grammar focused on in the chapter as well as introduce students to the academic content areas covered in the Structure and Written Expression section. The level of difficulty in these initial passages is lower than that of the reading passages in the Vocabulary and Reading Comprehension section of the TOEFL® Test, since their aim is not to improve reading skills but to provide a context for the grammar focused on in the chapter and make the grammar section of the exam more engaging and interesting for the student.

Structure of Each Chapter

INTRODUCTION

The Reading passage focuses on the grammar area of the chapter and at the same time covers a content area of the TOEFL® Test through a subject of general interest. Exercises based on the reading passage introduce and reinforce the structure or grammar area focused on in the chapter.

FOCUS ON GRAMMAR AREA

This part covers one of the grammar areas tested in the Structure and Written Expression section of the TOEFL® Test. The examples and exercises are related in subject matter to the content area of the chapter. Strategies are given throughout this part.

ON THE TOEFL® TEST

This part focuses on the identification of errors found on the TOEFL® Test, giving specific examples.

EXERCISES ON GRAMMAR FOCUS AREA

This part provides practice with TOEFL® Test-type questions on the grammar area focused on in the chapter. Items are in areas of mixed content.

TO THE STUDENT

Peterson's *TOEFL® Grammar Flash* will prepare you for Section 2, Structure and Written Expression, of the TOEFL® Test. The book is designed for both self-study and use in a classroom with a teacher. In sixteen chapters it covers all the main areas of grammar tested in this section of the test and provides you with simple explanations, TOEFL® Test-type examples, and practice. For further practice there are five Structure and Written Expression practice tests in Part II of the book. You can check your answers to the exercises in the book and the practice tests in the Answer Key at the back of the book.

As well as preparing you for the types of errors that are tested in the Structure and Written Expression section of the TOEFL® Test, this book introduces and familiarizes you with the major content areas that appear on the TOEFL® Test. These content areas are physical sciences, social sciences, and the arts and humanities.

I hope this book will make the content areas and grammar more interesting and accessible to you.

STRUCTURE AND WRITTEN EXPRESSION

The Structure and Written Expression Section of the TOEFL® Test

Section 2 of the TOEFL® Test tests your understanding of English grammar. The section is divided into two parts, with a different type of question in each part:

A: Structure (questions 1-15) tests sentence completion.
B: Written Expression (questions 16-40) tests error identification.

The number of items in the Structure and Written Expression parts are as follows:

	Short Form	Long Form
Structure	15	23
Written Expression	25	37
Total	40	60
Time	25 minutes	35 minutes

- **Language:** Section 2 tests standard written English. The language in this section is more formal than the language in the listening Comprehension section. There will be no contractions (there's) or idiomatic expressions.
- **Topics:** The topics in Section 2 are about academic subjects: the physical sciences (astronomy, geology), social sciences (anthropology, nutrition), or the arts and humanities (music, art). But you do not have to know about these subjects to answer the questions.

There are cultural references to the United States and Canada. These references may be to people, places, or things related to the United States and Canada, but you do not have to know any of these references or facts. All you have to do is concentrate on the structure of the sentence. A knowledge of the facts referred to in this section are entirely irrelevant to your score.

- **Grammar points tested:** Although a wide range of grammar points is tested, certain grammar points occur over and over again. Each chapter of this text concentrates on a particular grammar point tested on the TOEFL® Test.

TACTICS

There are two ways of answering the questions appearing on the TOEFL® Test.

1. *By analyzing the grammar of a sentence:* In the Structure part you can analyze the part that is missing, and in the Written Expression part the incorrect underlined item can be worked out.

2. *By using your intuition:* Some people "feel" an answer is right or wrong, although they may not know the grammar. This way may work for a person who has learned English by listening and speaking.

STRATEGIES FOR STRUCTURE AND WRITTEN EXPRESSION

- *Familiarize yourself with the directions* for both parts so you do not waste time reading the directions and examples.
- *Answer every item.* If you do not know the answer, do not leave a blank space. Always guess, even if you do not know. Wrong answers will not count against you. You can use a "guess" letter. A guess letter is one letter, A, B, C, or D, that you can use to answer all the items you do not know. You are more likely to get some correct if you use the same letter through the whole test than if you change letters all the time.
- *Use your time carefully.* Always read the four choices, even if they seem easy. You may make a careless mistake by answering a question too quickly. Don't lose time thinking about something you do not know. Mark the item lightly on your answer sheet so you can go back to it later. Go on to the next item. You should not spend more than thirty seconds per item.

STRUCTURE AND WRITTEN EXPRESSION

Strategies for Structure: Questions 1–15

This part of the test consists of fifteen incomplete sentences. A part of each sentence is replaced by a blank. Under each sentence four choices are listed, A, B, C, and D. One of the choices logically and grammatically completes the sentence.

- *Look at the answer choices first.*
  - If they are short, you can get an idea of what to look for when you read the sentence.
  - If they are long, read the sentence (stem) first. Analyze its structure. Work out how many clauses there are. See if the clauses have subjects and verbs. Look for connectors that join the clauses. Then look at the four choices. If you still do not know the answer, eliminate as many distractors as you can and take a guess from your remaining choices.

- *Read all the choices.* Never choose an answer before reading all four choices. Some of the choices may be very similar, and you may make a careless mistake.

- *Read the sentence completely with the answer you have chosen.* Make sure your answer fits. If the answer does not sound right, it may not be. If you do not know, guess and go on. If you have time you can come back to the difficult items later.

- *Watch for the following when you insert your answer into the sentence:*
  - Your answer may have an unnecessary word or phrase.
  - It may be incomplete.
  - It may be ungrammatical. If so, discard that answer and reconsider the remaining three.

- *Use your time carefully.* Do not spend so much time that you will not have enough time to finish the Written Expression part. Budget your time carefully. Do not spend more than thirty seconds on each item.

Strategies for Written Expression: Questions 16-30

This part of the test consists of twenty-five sentences. Each sentence has four words or phrases, A, B, C and D that are underlined. You must identify the incorrect word or phrase.

- *Read the complete sentence quickly.* Do not read just the underlined words or phrases. The underlined words or phrases may be correct on their own but incorrect in the context of the sentence.

- *The error will always be underlined.* Do not look for errors in other parts of the sentence. The rest of the sentence will only provide you with the clues to help you find the error.

- If you cannot find the error, go through a mental checklist of the most common types of errors (see the following table for a list of common errors) and see whether one of the underlined parts fits into one of the categories.

- If you still cannot find the error, eliminate the parts that seem correct, and then take a guess from your remaining options.

Most Common Errors in Written Expression*

Error Category	Frequency
Word form	21%
Word choice	15
Verbs	12
Parallel structure	9
Pronouns	7
Singular/plural nouns	6
Verbals (infinitives, gerunds, participles)	6
Prepositions	6
Articles	5
Comparative and superlatives	4
Word order	4
Conjunctions	2
Redundancy	1
Other types of errors	2

*Based on Bruce Roger's analysis of 20 different exams that test takers were allowed to keep after Disclosed Test Admission.

PART 1

Types of Structure and Written Expression Questions

CHAPTER 1 NOUNS

Introduction: The Brain

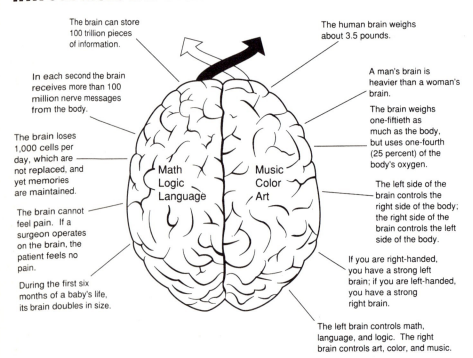

The brain can store 100 trillion pieces of information.

In each second the brain receives more than 100 million nerve messages from the body.

The brain loses 1,000 cells per day, which are not replaced, and yet memories are maintained.

The brain cannot feel pain. If a surgeon operates on the brain, the patient feels no pain.

During the first six months of a baby's life, its brain doubles in size.

The human brain weighs about 3.5 pounds.

A man's brain is heavier than a woman's brain.

The brain weighs one-fiftieth as much as the body, but uses one-fourth (25 percent) of the body's oxygen.

The left side of the brain controls the right side of the body; the right side of the brain controls the left side of the body.

If you are right-handed, you have a strong left brain; if you are left-handed, you have a strong right brain.

The left brain controls math, language, and logic. The right brain controls art, color, and music.

EXERCISE 1

Nouns are tested on the TOEFL® Test. Complete the sentences with nouns.

1. The brain stores 100 trillion pieces of _____.
2. Men's brains are heavier than _____ brains.
3. The brain uses one-quarter, or _____, of the body's oxygen.
4. The left brain controls math, _____, and _____.
5. The right brain controls color, _____, and _____.
6. The human brain weighs about 3.5 _____.
7. The brain cannot feel _____.
8. The brain receives more than 100 _____ _____ messages from the body.

EXERCISE 2

From the reading, work out whether these statements are true or false. Check T for true and F for false.

1. The weight of the brain depends on intelligence. T F
2. A jazz musician has a dominant right brain. T F
3. A left-handed person has a dominant left brain. T F
4. When you play a game of chess, you use the left side of your brain. T F
5. Your lost brain cells are always replaced. T F
6. The brain feels pain when you have a headache. T F

Grammar: Singular and Plural Nouns

Nouns can be classified into two groups: count nouns, which can be counted and which take an *s*, and noncount nouns, which cannot be counted and which usually do not take an *s*

> **STRATEGY**
>
> Look for a noncount noun that is pluralized where it generally should not be.

Look at the following table:

	Singular	**Plural**
Count noun	a cell one cell	cells two cells some cells a lot of cells many cells
Noncount noun	information some information a lot of information much information	

Count nouns
1. Take ***a/an*** or **one** in the singular.
2. Usually take a final **s/es** in the plural.

Noncount nouns
1. Do not take ***a/an*** in the singular.
2. Do not generally have a plural form.

Some count nouns are irregular and do not take an *s* in the plural. Here are some common irregular count nouns:

man—men	foot—feet
woman—women	tooth—teeth
child—children	fish—fish

Noncount nouns cannot be counted because they come in a mass or in an uncountable form. Nouns such as *blood, music,* and *excitement* cannot be counted. The following is a short list of some noncount nouns:

Food:	rice, sugar, fruit, milk, bread, butter, cheese
Fluids:	blood, water, oil, coffee, tea, gasoline
Raw materials:	wood, paper, glass, iron, silver, wool
Gases:	oxygen, nitrogen, air, pollution, steam
General:	furniture, mail, money, traffic, equipment
Groups:	jewelry, machinery, luggage, clothing, cash
Languages:	English, Chinese, Japanese, Spanish
Academic subjects:	chemistry, mathematics, psychology
Abstract things:	education, health, intelligence, beauty, knowledge, sleep, hope, music, time

QUANTIFIERS

A quantifier is a word that indicates an amount or quantity.

1. Some quantifiers are used only with plural count nouns.

   both   many   a few   several   fewer

   *They are controlled by **several** nerves.*
   *We have **fewer** cells as we get older.*

2. Some quantifiers are used only with singular count nouns.

   another   each   every

   ***Each** gland has a different purpose.*
   ***Every** muscle has its own group of nerves.*

3. Some quantifiers are used only with noncount nouns.

   a little   much   less   amount

   *The **amount** of oxygen available to the brain is important.*
   *If your brain gets **less** oxygen than it needs, you could become unconscious.*

4. Some quantifiers are used with both plural count nouns and noncount nouns.

all	plenty of	any
a lot of	enough	most
lots of	some	more

   *Brain cells use up **a lot** of energy.*
   ***Most** animals rely on instinct.*

Exercise 3

Correct the errors in noun forms in the following sentences.

1. Intelligence is the ability to use thought and knowledges to understand things and solve problems.
2. Hormones help adjust the mixture of sugar, salt, and waters in your body.
3. *Psychology*, meaning the study of the mind and how it works, comes from a Greek word meaning lifes or soul.
4. Brain cells use up a lot of energy, so they need a constant supply of oxygens.
5. Each hemisphere of the brain receives informations about the opposite side of the visual field.
6. Although millions of brain neurons are active at any one time, they do not use much electric powers.
7. Lights entering the eye forms an image on 130 million tiny light cells.
8. Most animal are not able to rely on learning and memory.

COMPOUND NOUNS

Strategy

Look for compound nouns in which both nouns are pluralized, instead of just the second noun.

Compound nouns are two nouns that are used together to make one word or idea. The first noun acts as an adjective to the second noun and usually does not take *s*. The second noun can be plural.

brain cell
brain wave
computer scientists

Compound nouns may also be used with number expressions.

> **Strategy**
>
> Beware of compound nouns with numbers, where the compound noun used as an adjective may be in the plural form!

*The brain uses as much power as a **ten-watt** lightbulb.* (noun used as an adjective)
*The brain uses as much power as a lightbulb of **ten watts**.* (noun used as a noun)
*He recited a **16,000-page** book from memory.* (noun used as an adjective)
*He recited a book of **16,000 pages** from memory.* (noun used as a noun)

NUMBERS

> **Strategy**
>
> When you see nouns involving numbers, such as *hundred, thousand,* or *million,* make sure that they are not in the plural form when they follow numbers.

Numbers such as *hundred, thousand, million,* and *trillion* are plural when there are no numbers before them.
The brain receives 100 million messages a second.
The brain stores trillions of messages.

EXERCISE 4

> **Correct the errors in the following sentences.**

1. People's brains weigh more now than they did 100 year ago.
2. Nerves impulses can travel at speeds of up to 488 feet per second.
3. The brain contains between 10 trillions and 100 trillions neurons.
4. Each neuron is linked by synapses to thousand of other neurons.
5. Nerves endings below the skin's surface pick up sensations of cold, heat, and touch.
6. There are three to four millions pain receptors in the skin.
7. A three-years-old child's brain is two-thirds the size it will finally be.
8. The brain uses 25 percents of the blood's oxygen.

On the TOEFL® Test

Nouns are tested in the Written Expression section of the exam. Check for the following types of errors with nouns.

1. A noncount noun may be pluralized.

    Example: In a person's lifetime, the brain can store 100 trillion
                                          A   B
            pieces of informations.
               C   D

    The correct answer is (D); *information* is a noncount noun and cannot be plural.

2. A plural noun may be used when the verb or phrase requires a singular noun.

    Example: Each part of the brains controls a separate part of the
                    A   B   C
            body.
             D

    The best answer is (B); a singular noun *brain* must be used with "part of the."

3. A singular noun may be used when the verb requires a plural noun.

    Example: Human brain are more powerful than those
                    A
            of other species because of their complex circuitry.
                  B   C   D

    The correct answer is (A); a plural noun *brains* must be used because the verb *are* is plural.

4. In compound nouns where two nouns are used together, both nouns may be pluralized instead of just the second noun.

    Example: Brains cells die at the rate of 100,000 per day by age 60, and
               A   B   C
            they are not replaced like other body cells.
                                      D

    The correct answer is (A); the correct form is *brain cells*.

5. In compound nouns involving numbers and measurements, the compound noun used as an adjective may be in the plural form.

   Example: Man's three-pounds brain is the most complex and orderly
               A   B
   arrangement of matter in the universe.
         C   D

   The best answer is (B); when a compound noun is used as an adjective, it is singular. Therefore the correct answer is *three-pound*.

6. When noun phrases involving a number such as *hundred, thousand,* or *million* follow another number, the plural form may be used.

   Example: The brain loses fifty thousands neurons a day and yet
                      A   B
   maintains its basic patterns and memories.
              C   D

   The best answer is (A); the singular form *thousand* should be used when it follows a number.

Exercises on Nouns

From the four underlined words or phrases (A), (B), (C), or (D), identify the *one* that is not correct.

1. The potato was the staple of Ireland, and when the crop failed in 1840,
       A   B   C
   there was mass starvations.
            D

2. Shark can maneuver considerably faster than other fish because they
    A   B C
   have no bones.
      D

3. Although sugar cane and sugar beet look very different, the sugars that is
              A   B   C
   refined from them tastes almost the same.
                               D

4. Textiles industries are as widespread as food industries because both
        A   B
   supply basic human needs.
       C   D

5. Many animal species are totally colorsblind, but the condition is very
         A   B   C
   rare in humans.
       D

6. Our skulls is made up of eight cranial and fourteen facial bones.
      A   B   C   D

7. Diamonds, which is about 40 times as hard as talc, is made up of
         A   B   C
   pure carbon.
       D

8. The oceans contain about 97 percent of the world's water supply, and
        A   B   C
   about another 2 percent of the world's water supply is ices.
                                                     D

9. Brain waves patterns vary among different people and in
           A   B   C
   different activities.
         D

10. The ancestor of today's horse was a little mammal called eohippus,
          A   B
    which first appeared 54 millions years ago.
                          C   D

11. Lasers are of great value in areas such as communications, industry,
      A   B
    medicine, and scientifics research.
        C   D

12. Dinosaurs are classified as reptiles, although some appear to have been
        A   B   C
    warms-blooded.
        D

CHAPTER 2 PRONOUNS

Introduction: Penguins

There are eighteen different kinds of penguins, and they all live south of the equator. The largest are the emperor penguins, which live in Antarctica. They lay their eggs about fifty miles from the coast. There the penguins have nothing to make a nest out of, but the eggs cannot be laid directly on the ice, or they would freeze. The emperor penguins have to take care of their eggs in a special way.

The female produces one egg. As soon as she lays her egg, the male penguin rolls it on top of his feet. A special fold of skin on the bottom of his stomach comes down over the egg to protect it from the cold. For two months the male penguins stand together to protect themselves from the cold with their eggs on their feet. They cannot move or eat.

The female goes to find food as soon as she lays her egg. Finally, after two months she returns and takes the egg from the male. The male penguin, which now has had no food for two months, returns to the sea.

After the egg is hatched, the female and the male take turns carrying the baby penguin on their feet. When the weather gets cold, the baby is covered by the fold of skin, which keeps it warm.

Exercise 1

Pronouns are tested on the TOEFL® Test. Answer the following questions using a pronoun.

1. Where do the emperor penguins live?
   _____

2. How many eggs does the female emperor produce at a time?
   _____

3. What does the male emperor penguin use to protect the egg from the cold?
   _____

4. Why do the male emperor penguins stand together?
   _____

5. Where do the males put their eggs when they stand together?
   _____

6. Where does the female go?
   _____

7. When does she return?
   _____

8. What does the male penguin do after she returns?
   _____

EXERCISE 2

> **From the reading, work out whether these statements are true or false. Check T for true and F for false.**

1. There are no penguins on the North Pole.   T F
2. All penguins live south of the equator.   T F
3. All penguins are the same.   T F
4. All penguins have folds under their abdomen.   T F
5. The fold of skin is used only to keep the egg warm.   T F
6. Only the female takes care of the penguin chick.   T F
7. Emperor penguins do not make nests.   T F
8. Emperor penguins lay their eggs very near the sea.   T F

Grammar: Pronouns

There are five forms of pronouns in English: subject pronouns, object pronouns, possessive pronouns, reflexive pronouns, and relative pronouns. Possessive adjectives will also be included in this chapter, although they are not pronouns.

> **Strategy**
>
> It is important to know the five forms of pronouns and the possessive adjectives that are often confused with them. Errors may include the use of one type or form of pronoun in place of another.

SUBJECT PRONOUNS

I	we
you	you
he/she/it	they

The subject pronoun is used

1. When it is the subject of a verb.
   They live south of the equator.
2. When the subjects of the two clauses are compared.
   They are more protected against the cold than *we* (are).
3. After the verb *to be*.
   It is *he* with the egg.
4. After *as* and *than*.
   She is not as tired as *he* (is).

Exercise 3

> **Circle the correct pronoun.**

1. It is she/her who goes to find food.
2. He/Him has the responsibility of incubating the egg.
3. She/Her lays one egg.
4. John is stronger than I/me.
5. He/Him and his father are both great explorers.
6. Are you sure that they/them are here?

OBJECT PRONOUNS

me	us
you	you
him/her/it	them

The object pronoun is used

1. When it is the direct object of a verb.

   *She gives **him** the egg.*

2. After prepositions.

   *When she returns, she takes over the egg from **him**.*

   But when the preposition introduces a new clause, the subject pronoun must be used because the pronoun is now the subject of the new clause.

   *He leaves after **she** returns.*

3. When the objects of two clauses are compared.

   *It is easier for **them** than **us**.*

Exercise 4

> **Correct the pronoun errors in the following sentences where necessary.**

1. He helps she take care of the baby penguin.
2. She lays her egg and then leaves.
3. They feed them until they can swim.
4. It is not easy for they to survive under such conditions.
5. It is harder for him than for she.
6. He goes to the sea after she returns.

POSSESSIVE ADJECTIVES

my	our
your	your
his/her/its	their

The possessive adjective is used.

1. To modify a noun and show ownership.

   *They lay **their** eggs about fifty miles from the coast.*

2. To refer to parts of the body.

   *The male penguin rolls the egg on top of **his** feet.*

3. To modify a gerund.

   *We are surprised by **their** nesting in such harsh conditions.*

Exercise 5

> **Complete the sentences with the correct pronoun.**

1. She lays _____ egg.
2. He has a special fold of skin on the bottom of _____ stomach.
3. They take care of _____ young in a special way.
4. It is protected from the cold by _____ father.
5. They keep the eggs on _____ feet.
6. The male penguin looks forward to _____ coming back from the sea.

POSSESSIVE PRONOUNS

mine	ours
yours	yours
his/hers/its	theirs

The possessive pronoun is used

1. To replace a possessive adjective and a noun.

   *She takes her turn, and he takes **his** (his turn).*

2. After the verb to be.

   *The egg is **hers**.*

3. After the preposition *of* when it means "one of many."

   *It is a habit of **theirs**.*

4. To replace the second possessive adjective and noun when they are being compared.

   *Their life seems more difficult than **ours**.*

Exercise 6

> **Circle the correct pronoun.**

1. It is an experiment of **his**/him.
2. The Adélie penguins live in a cold climate, but the emperor penguins live in a harsher climate than them/**theirs**.
3. Seven nations claim that Antarctica is their/**theirs**.
4. The researcher in the picture is a friend of **ours**/us.
5. His research was good but her/**hers** is better.
6. Studying penguins is a hobby of **mine**/my.

REFLEXIVE PRONOUNS

myself	ourselves
yourself	yourselves
himself/herself/itself	themselves

The reflexive pronoun is used

1. To emphasize the subject noun or pronoun it refers to and to emphasize the fact that the subject did the action alone.

   *He takes care of the egg **himself**.*
   Or: *He **himself** takes care of the egg.*

2. As the object of a verb when the subject and object are the same.

   *They stand together to protect **themselves** from the cold.*

3. As the object of the preposition by when the subject did the action alone.

   *The penguin chick is unable to get food by **itself**.*

Exercise 7

Complete the sentences with the correct reflexive pronoun.

1. Penguins push _____ along the ice using their flippers.
2. To protect _____ from the cold, the penguin has a layer of fat under its feathers.
3. The female lays her egg and walks back to the sea by _____.
4. During the two months the male penguin cannot feed _____.
5. The male penguin _____ incubates the egg.
6. Since humans do not have the insulation that penguins do, we cannot protect _____ from such temperatures without special clothing.

RELATIVE PRONOUNS

The relative pronouns in English are *who, whom, whose, which,* and *that.*

> **Strategy**
> It is important to make sure that the relative pronoun agrees with the subject.

Who refers to people and household animals.

Whom refers to people and household animals. It is used in the object position in formal written English or with *who* plus a preposition in spoken English.

Whose refers to people, animals, and things. It shows possession.

Which refers to things, collective nouns, and animals.

That refers to people, animals, and things.

Exercise 8

> **Correct relative pronoun errors where necessary in the following sentences.**

1. There are eighteen different kinds of penguins whom live south of the equator.

2. The biologist which went to the South Pole is studying emperor penguins.

3. Emperor penguins survive winds who blow at speeds of up to ninety-five miles an hour in winter.

4. Emperor penguins, whose nesting ground is fifty miles inland from the coast, have a special way of incubating their eggs.

5. Emperor penguins, who are the largest among penguins, do not make nests.

6. The United States has sent researchers to Antarctica which are making experiments to measure the energy expended by emperor penguins.

On the TOEFL® Test

Pronouns are tested in the Written Expression section of the exam. Check for the following types of errors with pronouns.

1. The incorrect pronoun form or type may be used. The possessive pronoun (hers) may be used instead of the possessive adjective (her).

    Example: The young emperor chick stands in front of one of it parents
                        A   B   C
    to be protected from the cold.
              D

    The best answer is (C); the possessive form *its* must be used, not the object form.

    Example: Some penguins they live in warmer places like to make
                                 A   B
    their nests in holes in the ground.
        C   D

    The correct answer is (A); the relative pronoun *which* or *that* must be used instead of the subject *they*.

2. The pronoun may not agree with the noun it refers to.

   Example: Sometimes <u>penguins slide</u> on <u>their stomachs</u>, pushing <u>itself</u>
                                    A   B   C
   with <u>their flippers</u>.
             D

   The correct answer is (C); The noun *penguins* is plural; therefore, the reflexive pronoun referring to penguins must also be plural. The correct answer is *themselves*.

   Example: Penguins <u>have special glands</u> <u>who remove</u> salt from the
                                     A   B
   water <u>they drink</u> and the food <u>they eat</u>.
           C   D

   The best answer is (B); the relative pronoun *who* refers to people. In this sentence, the referent is *glands*; therefore, either *that* or *which* should be used.

3. Pronouns that are not necessary may be included.

   Example: The <u>male Adélie penguin</u> <u>which may not</u> leave <u>the nest</u> until
                              A   B   C
   <u>his mate</u> returns.
       D

   The correct answer is (B); the relative pronoun *which* is not necessary in this sentence because there is only one verb, *leave*.

   Example: <u>Under the feathers</u> is a layer of fat <u>that</u> <u>it</u> protects
                      A   B C
   <u>the penguin</u> from the cold.
        D

   The best answer is (C); the pronoun *it* is not necessary.

Exercises on Pronouns

> From the four underlined words or phrases (A), (B), (C), or (D), identify the *one* that is not correct.

1. The penguin chicks cannot go into the water to get themselves own
       A   B
   food until they have waterproof coats of feathers like their parents.
              C   D

2. Balloons rise into the air because they contain a gas who is less dense,
            A   B   C
   or lighter, than air.
      D

3. The narwhal is the only animal in the world that has a tusk on
                    A   B
   only one side of it body.
                  C   D

4. Silver is too soft to use by itself, so it is mixed with another metal to
                              A   B   C
   make themselves harder.
        D

5. Most slugs and snails breathe using a lung which opens through a small
                         A   B
   hole in the side of its bodies.
        C   D

6. Every fuel has their own particular temperature at which it begins to
              A   B   C   D
   burn.

7. Harriet Tubman, she an escaped slave, led more than
                   A
   three hundred slaves to freedom on the Underground Railroad.
         B   C   D

8. Dreaming, like all other mental processes, it is a product of the brain
            A   B   C
   and its activity.
       D

9. Snails produce a colorless, sticky discharge that forms a protective
                   A   B
   carpet under them as their travel along.
         C   D

10. George Washington Carver <u>won international</u> fame for
                              A
    <u>his agricultural research</u>, <u>who involved</u> <u>extensive work</u> with peanuts.
              B   C   D

11. Enzymes <u>enable the smallest virus</u> to enter <u>cells</u> <u>in order to</u>
                      A   B   C
    <u>reproduce themselves</u>.
              D

12. Jack London, <u>whom was known</u> for <u>his stories of Alaska</u>, <u>lived there</u>
                        A   B   C
    during the <u>Klondike gold rush</u>.
                      D

CHAPTER 3: PARTS OF A SENTENCE

Introduction: Phyllis Wheatley

Phyllis Wheatley was kidnapped from Africa at the age of eight. She was brought to Boston in 1761, a sickly child only able to speak Senegalese. At the age of thirteen she wrote her first poem. In 1773 her first book of poems was published, the second volume of poetry published by a woman in America.

At the Boston slave market, Phyllis was purchased by John Wheatley, a tailor whose wife, impressed by the child's aptitude, taught her to speak, read, and write English. In a few years Phyllis had also learned geography, history, and Latin and had developed a liking for classical poets such as Horace and Virgil. Her first poem, a translation from the Latin of Ovid, so amazed the literary circles in Boston that they had it published. In 1768 she wrote "To the King's Most Excellent Health," and in 1772 she composed a poem to her mistress, who was so moved that she freed Phyllis and sent her to England to regain her health.

With the London publication of her book, *Poems on Various Subjects, Religious and Moral,* her fame spread on both sides of the Atlantic, and she became a celebrity.

EXERCISE 1

> **The various parts that make up a sentence are tested on the TOEFL® Test. Underline the subject and circle the verb in the following sentences.**

1. At the Boston slave market, Phyllis was purchased by John Wheatley.
2. In a few years, Phyllis had learned geography, history, and Latin.
3. Her mistress, Mrs. Wheatley, was impressed by the child's aptitude.
4. At the age of thirteen, she wrote her first poem.
5. In 1773 her first book of poems was published.
6. With the London publication of her book, her fame spread on both sides of the Atlantic.

Exercise 2

> In some sentences the verb agrees with the subject; in some sentences the verb does not agree with the subject. Write *C* for correct and *NC* for not correct.

1. Phyllis Wheatley was kidnapped from Africa.
2. History, geography, and Latin was the subjects she learned.
3. Classical poets such as Horace and Virgil were Phillis's favorites.
4. Phillis was purchased by Mr. Wheatley, whose wife were impressed by her and taught her to speak English.
5. The literary circles in Boston were impressed by her poem.
6. On both sides of the Atlantic her poetry was famous.

Grammar: Parts of a Sentence

The clause has a subject and a verb. It can stand independently or alone.

1. A **simple sentence** contains a single clause.

   <u>She</u>   <u>wrote</u>   <u>a book</u>
   subject   *verb*   *object*

2. A **compound sentence** contains two independent clauses joined by a conjunction (such as *and* or *but*).

   <u>At age thirteen she wrote her first poem</u>
                 independent clause
     <u>and</u>
   conjunction
   <u>in 1773 she wrote her first book.</u>
             independent clause

3. A **complex sentence** contains an independent (main) clause and a dependent (subordinate) clause. The subordinate clause may be a noun clause, an adverb clause, or an adjective clause.

Main clause	Subordinate clause	Noun clause (that, what, how . . .) Adverb clause (because, although, if . . .) Adjective clause (who, which, where . . .)

Her mistress realized <u>that Phyllis was talented</u>.
　　　　　　　　　　　　　　　noun clause
She wrote a poem for her mistress, <u>who was very impressed</u>.
　　　　　　　　　　　　　　　　　　　　adjective clause
She went to England <u>because she had health problems</u>.
　　　　　　　　　　　　　adverb clause

The three types of subordinate clauses are dealt with in Chapters 7, 8, and 9.

SUBJECT AND VERB

A clause has a subject and a verb. Some verbs (action verbs) take an object.

<u>She</u>	<u>wrote</u>	<u>a book</u>.
subject	verb	object

The Verb
The verb may be a single word (*wrote* in the previous example) or a verb phrase with one or more auxiliary verbs and a main verb (*would have written*). The verb may be in active form (*wrote*) or passive form (*was written*). See Chapter 4, on verbs.

The Subject
A subject may consist of one or more nouns or a phrase:

Noun: **Phyllis** *wrote her first poem at the age of thirteen.*
Phrase: **The first black woman poet in America** *produced her first book in 1773.*

The subject may take various forms:

1. A noun:
   The woman *wrote a book.*
2. A pronoun:
   She *wrote a book.*
3. A clause:
   What she wrote *amazed everyone.*
4. A gerund:
   Writing *was her talent.*
5. A gerund phrase:
   Writing poetry *was her talent.*
6. An infinitive:
   To write *requires special talent.*
7. An infinitive phrase:
   To write poetry *in Latin requires special talent.*

> **Strategy**
>
> There is only one subject in a clause. Be aware that on the test, the subject may be repeated. This is an error.
>
> Correct: Phyllis Wheatley wrote poetry books.
> Error: Phyllis Wheatley *she* wrote poetry books.

SUBJECT AND VERB AGREEMENT

The subject and verb must agree in person and number.

> **Strategy**
>
> Subject and verb agreement often presents difficulty to some learners of English since there are some subjects that take singular verbs and others that take plural verbs.

Subjects Taking a Singular Verb

1. Subjects with the following prepositional phrases take a singular verb:

as well as	together with
along with	in addition to
accompanied by	among

   *Among her works **is** To the King's Most Excellent Health.*

2. When the words below are used as subjects they take a singular verb:

one	each	any *plus singular noun*	some *plus singular noun*	every
nobody	either	anybody	somebody	everybody
no one	neither	anyone	someone	everyone
nothing		anything	something	everything

   ***Everyone was** amazed by her poems.*

3. When *it* introduces a sentence, *it* takes a singular verb.

   ***It was** her poems that amazed everyone.*

Subjects Taking a Plural Verb

1. When subjects are joined by *and* or *both . . . and,* the verb is plural.

   Both *her mother* **and** *father* **were** *proud.*

2. The words *several, both, many,* and *few* always take a plural verb.

   Many were *amazed by her talent.*

Subjects Taking Either a Singular or a Plural Verb

1. *A number of* takes a plural verb, but *the number of* takes a singular verb.

   A number of people **were** *at the reading.*
   The number of people at the banquet **was** *amazing.*

2. The words below take a singular or plural verb depending on the noun that follows them:

   none   no   all   some
   most   half   any   majority

   All of her **poems were** *good.*
   All of her **work was** *good.*

3. When subjects are joined by *either . . . or, neither . . . nor,* or *not only . . . but also,* the verb is singular or plural depending on the subject nearest to it.

   Not only her master but also **her mistress was** *proud of her.*
   Not only her mistress but also the literary **circles were** *amazed by her talent.*

Exercise 3

Choose the option (A), (B), (C), or (D) that best completes the sentence.

1. During the war _____ wrote a poem for General Washington, who complimented her on her "style and manner."
   (A) Phyllis Wheatley was
   (B) it was Phyllis Wheatley
   (C) Phyllis Wheatley
   (D) Phyllis Wheatley she

2. _____ was initially by horse or foot in the colonial period.
   (A) It was land travel
   (B) Land travel
   (C) That land travel
   (D) Because land travel

3. In 1736, the number of poor people in Boston receiving public assistance _____ about 4,000.
   (A) was
   (B) were
   (C) it was
   (D) they were

4. _____, Jupiter Hannon, was the first American black to publish his own verse.
   (A) He was a poet and Baptist preacher of Long Island
   (B) The poet and Baptist preacher of Long Island
   (C) The poet and Baptist preacher of Long Island he was
   (D) The poet and he was a Baptist preacher of Long Island

5. Outstanding for his talent as an essayist, inventor, mathematician, and astrologer in the 1770s _____, who also published a popular almanac.
   (A) were Benjamin Banneker
   (B) it was Benjamin Banneker
   (C) was Benjamin Banneker
   (D) Benjamin Banneker

6. During the eighteenth century, communication within and between cities _____ at first.
   (A) were difficult
   (B) they were difficult
   (C) difficult
   (D) was difficult

IT AND THERE

> **Strategy**
>
> Some sentences or clauses begin with *it* or *there*. Be aware of the constructions that follow these subjects. In the Structure section parts of a sentence including *it* and *there* may be omitted.

A sentence or clause may begin with the words *it* or *there*.
It is used in three ways:

1. *It* is used as subject followed by the verb *to be:*

   It was in 1761 that she came to Boston. (*It* + to be + *that.* . . .)

2. *It* is used as subject when the information is related to an adjective:

   It was important to be free. (*It* + to be + adjective + infinitive)

3. *It* is used as a subject when it is used with a time phrase:

   It took her a few years to learn English. (*It* + *take* + time phrase + infinitive)

There shows that something or someone exists at a special time or place. In this use, the word *there* follows this construction:

there + to be + subject

> *There are many books about Phyllis Wheatley today.*
> *There were not many famous women poets in the 1770s.*

EXERCISE 4

> **Circle the letter of the word that best completes the sentence.**

1. _____ not a single hard-surfaced road during the entire colonial period aside from city streets.

   (A) It was
   (B) There was
   (C) It
   (D) There were

2. _____ in 1776 that the Declaration of Independence was signed.

   (A) It was
   (B) There was
   (C) There
   (D) It

3. _____ more than 300,000 people in Philadelphia by the end of the colonial period, making it the largest city in the colonies.

   (A) There was
   (B) It was
   (C) They were
   (D) There were

4. In the eighteenth century, _____ not many women who had access to formal education in the colonies.

   (A) there were
   (B) it was
   (C) were
   (D) were there

5. After the Revolution, although some advances were made in education, _____ a slow process.

   (A) they were
   (B) it
   (C) it was
   (D) there was

On the TOEFL® Test

> **Parts of a sentence are tested in the Structure section, where any part of the sentence may be missing. The subject, the verb, or both may be missing.**

Example: Postal service _____ almost nonexistent in the colonies.

   (A) that was
   (B) was
   (C) it was
   (D) being

The best answer is (B); (A) is incorrect because *that* is needed only to connect a relative clause to an independent clause, and in this case there is only one clause. (C) is incorrect because it repeats the subject. (D) is incorrect because the *-ing* form cannot be the main verb of a clause.

Example: _____ twenty-two colonial newspapers by 1775.

   (A) About
   (B) About were
   (C) Were about
   (D) There were about

The correct answer is (D); (A) is incorrect because it lacks a verb. (B) is incorrect because there is no subject. (C) is incorrect because it has the wrong word order.

Exercises on Parts of a Sentence

From the four words or phrases (A), (B), (C), or (D), choose the one that best completes the sentence.

1. _____ in fluorescent lamps, television tubes, and other devices.
   - (A) Phosphors are used
   - (B) It is phosphors
   - (C) To use phosphors
   - (D) Using phosphors

2. The tips of some undersea mountains _____ islands in the middle of the ocean.
   - (A) to form
   - (B) they form
   - (C) form
   - (D) forming

3. _____ of fish: jawless fish, cartilaginous fish, and bony fish.
   - (A) It is three types
   - (B) There are three types
   - (C) Three types
   - (D) Three types are

4. _____ to stop yourself from blinking except for a short period of time.
   - (A) Impossible it
   - (B) Impossible
   - (C) It impossible
   - (D) It is impossible

5. _____ the sitka spruce a hundred years to grow eleven inches.
   - (A) It takes
   - (B) To take
   - (C) By taking
   - (D) That takes

6. _____ today was developed by the Swiss scientist Horace de Sassure around 1773.
   - (A) Mountaineering it as we know
   - (B) Mountaineering as we know it
   - (C) We know mountaineering is
   - (D) We know there is mountaineering

7. _____ of the surface of the Earth is covered by water.
   - (A) Three-quarters is nearly
   - (B) There is nearly three-quarters
   - (C) It is nearly three-quarters
   - (D) Nearly three-quarters

8. By the mid-eighteenth century _____ so many new immigrants entering North America from Europe that the original colonies in the Northeast were overcrowded.
   - (A) it were
   - (B) were
   - (C) there
   - (D) there were

9. _____ not until the end of the seventeenth century that scientists began to stress the importance of experiment as a way of gaining knowledge.

(A) There was
(B) It was
(C) There
(D) It

10. _____ are the most poisonous fish in the world.

(A) There are stonefish
(B) That the stonefish
(C) They are the stonefish
(D) Stonefish

11. Seismic prospecting _____ used to map out rock structures below the ground.

(A) widely
(B) are widely
(C) is widely
(D) it is widely

12. _____ in space, a rocket has to be powerful enough to break out of the pull of the Earth's gravity.

(A) To travel
(B) It is travel
(C) That travel
(D) Travel

CHAPTER 4: VERBS

Introduction: The Olympics

The word "olympic" comes from the name of the town Olympia in Greece, where the ancient Olympic Games were always held. The first recorded Olympic Games were held in 776 B.C.; the Games took place every fourth year after that date until they were abolished by a Roman emperor in A.D. 394.

It was not until 1875, when archeologists discovered the ruins of the Olympic Stadium in Greece, that interest in the Games was renewed. Baron Pierre de Coubertin, a French scholar and educator, proposed that the Games should be revived as an international competition to encourage both sport and world peace.

The first modern Olympic Games were held in Athens in 1896. Like their classical predecessors, the athletes were men only; women were admitted to the Games in 1900. Since that time, the Games have been held at four-year intervals as in ancient Greece. However, since de Coubertin's dream of world peace has not been realized, the two World Wars prevented those of 1916, 1940, and 1944 from being held.

The Olympic Games have been confined to amateur athletes despite a few recent exceptions. There are pressures on the Olympic authorities to admit other professionals to the Games. Such a step would damage the entire concept of the Olympics. The following words appear on the scoreboard at every Olympic opening: "The most important thing is not to win but to take part." In contrast, the aim of every professional is to win.

EXERCISE 1

> **Verb forms are tested on the TOEFL® Test.**

Complete the sentences with the correct form of the verb in parentheses.

1. The word "olympic" (come) _____ from Olympia in Greece.
2. In A.D. 394, a Roman emperor (abolish) _____ the Olympic Games.
3. In 1875 archeologists (discover) _____ the ruins of the Olympic Stadium in Greece.

4. The French educator Pierre de Coubertin (propose) _____ that the Games be revived.

5. Since 1896 the Olympic Games (be held) _____ every four years with some exceptions.

6. In the Olympic Games of 1896 the athletes (be) _____ men only.

7. Women (be admitted) _____ in 1900.

Exercise 2

Correct the verb tenses in the following sentences where necessary.

1. The Olympics have taken place every four years between 776 B.C. and A.D. 394.

2. Women started to participate in the Games in 1900.

3. From 1896 to the present, the Olympic Games were held every four years.

4. With a few recent exceptions, professional athletes do not take part in the Olympic Games.

5. With this international competition, Pierre de Coubertin has wanted to encourage both sport and world peace.

6. In 1916, 1940, and 1944 the Olympic Games have not taken place.

Grammar: Verbs

Verbs are tested in both the Structure and the Written Expression sections of the exam.

Strategy

It is important to:

1. Recognize the verb in a sentence (the verb is the action). Words that look like verbs such as gerunds, infinitives, and participles are not verbs.
2. Check if the verb agrees with the subject (see Chapter 3).
3. Check if the tense of the verb is correct. The time words and the context will help you do this.

TENSES

The following tables review verb tenses:

Usage	Examples
Present Continuous Tense	
1. An activity that is in progress at the moment	Mary is watching TV right now.
2. A general activity that takes place this week, this month, or this year	I'm training for the Olympics.
3. Future arrangements	I'm going to Sweden next winter.
Simple Present Tense	
1. A habitual action	I run every morning.
2. A general fact	The sun rises in the east.
3. Future timetables	The ticket office opens at 9:00.
Simple Past Tense	
1. An action that began and ended at a specific time in the past	We won a gold medal last year.
2. An action that occurred over a period of time and was completed in the past	She skated for fifteen years.
3. An activity that took place regularly in the past	She trained every morning before work.

Usage	Examples

Past Continuous Tense

1. An interrupted action — I was watching the Olympics on TV, when he walked in.
2. A repeated or continuous state in the past — I was making many new friends at the Olympic Village.

Future Tense (going to)

1. Expressing a prior plan — My brother is going to go with me next week.
2. Predicting something that is likely to happen in the future — We are going to win. I know it.

Future Tense (will)

1. Predicting something that is likely to happen in the future — You will win the race. I know it.
2. Expressing willingness to do something — I will go with you if you like.
3. Making a decision at the time of speaking — I will call you in a few minutes then.

Future Continuous Tense

1. An action that will be continuing at a particular time in the future — This time next week I will be training for the race.

Present Perfect Tense

1. An action that happened at an unspecified time in the past — I have seen him on television.
2. An action that has happened recently — She has just gone out.
3. An action that began in the past and continues in the present (usually with "for" or "since") — She has been training for two years.
4. Repetition of an action before now — He has been to the Olympics several times.

Present Perfect Continuous Tense

1. Expressing the duration of an action that began in the past and continues in the present (with "for," "since," "all morning," "all day") — John has been swimming for two hours.

Usage	Examples
2. A general action in progress recently for which no specific time is mentioned	I have been thinking about competing next year.
3. An action that began in the past and has just recently ended	Have you been crying? Your eyes are red.

Past Perfect Tense

1. A past action that occurred before another action in the past	She had just left when I arrived there.
2. An action that was expected to occur in the past	I had hoped to get their decision before today.

Past Perfect Continuous Tense

1. Expressing the duration of an activity that occurred before another action in the past year	She had been competing for six years before she tried out for the Olympics last year.
2. An action occurring recently before another action in the past	He looked tired because he had been running for six hours.

Future Perfect Tense

1. An action that will be completed before a particular time in the future	By next June I will have participated in four Olympics.

Future Perfect Continuous Tense

1. Expressing the duration of time that has occurred before a specific time in the future	By next May I will have been training at this gym for eleven years.

MODALS

A modal is always followed by the base form of a verb.
The following is a list of some modals:

| can | may | will | shall | must | had better |
| could | might | would | should | have to | ought to |

A modal expresses mood or attitude:

    Ability: She **can** run in the race.
    Possibility: She **could** run in the race.
                         She **might** run in the race.
                         She **may** run in the race.
    Advisability: She **had better** run in the race.
                         She **ought to** run in the race.
                         She **should** run in the race.

Necessity:	She **must** run in the race.
	She **has to** run in the race.
Intention:	She **shall** run in the race.
	She **will** run in the race.
Past Habit:	She **would** run in the race.

Strategy

Remember the correct word order for modals.

Correct word order: *She would run in the race.* Incorrect word order: *She run would in the race.*

EXERCISE 3

Circle the letter of the word or phrase that correctly completes the sentence.

1. When archeologists discovered the ruins of the Olympic Stadium, interest in the Games _____.

    (A) was renewed
    (B) were renewed
    (C) they were renewed
    (D) renewed

2. The ancient Olympic Games _____ as amateur contests, but in time became professional.

    (A) begun
    (B) began
    (C) beginning
    (D) they began

3. The Olympic Games are held every four years in a selected country, and _____ to athletes of all nations.

    (A) they are opened
    (B) are opened
    (C) they are open
    (D) it is open

4. Winning first place in an event was the only glory in the ancient Games because second and third places _____.

    (A) did not recognize
    (B) are not recognized
    (C) was not recognized
    (D) were not recognized

5. The winners received a wreath _____ from the branches of the sacred olive tree.
   (A) made
   (B) was made
   (C) making
   (D) to make

6. After more than 1,500 years, Athens _____ for the site of the first modern Olympics.
   (A) were chosen
   (B) was chosen
   (C) is chosen
   (D) chosen

7. The marathon, first staged in 1896, _____ the legendary feat of a Greek soldier who carried news of victory from the battlefield at Marathon to Athens.
   (A) was commemorated
   (B) commemorated
   (C) commemorates
   (D) commemorating

8. The Olympic torch _____ throughout the Games and is then extinguished at the closing ceremony.
   (A) burning
   (B) is burned
   (C) burned
   (D) burns

PASSIVE VOICE

> **Strategy**
>
> A frequent error is to use an active verb instead of a passive or a passive instead of an active. Remember that if the subject does the action, the verb is active; if the subject receives the action, the verb is passive.

The passive is formed by *be* + a verb ending in *ed* (past participle or an irregular past participle). In a passive sentence, the object of an active verb becomes the subject of the passive verb. The passive is used when the person or the thing done is more important, or when the agent who did the action is not known.
*Active: Archeologists **discovered** the ruins.*
*Passive: The ruins **were discovered** by archeologists.*

The following table shows how to form the passive:

Active Voice	Passive Voice
1. The flame *opens* the Games.	The Games *are opened* by the flame.
2. The flame *is opening* the Games.	The Games *are being opened* by the flame.
3. The flame *has opened* the Games.	The Games *have been opened* by the flame.

Active Voice	Passive Voice
4. The flame *opened* the Games.	The Games *were opened* by the flame.
5. The flame *was opening* the Games.	The Games *were being opened* by the flame.
6. The flame *had opened* the Games.	The Games *had been opened* by the flame.
7. The flame *will open* the Games.	The Games *will be opened* by the flame.
8. The flame *is going to open* the Games.	The Games *are going to be opened* by the flame.
9. The flame *will have opened* the Games.	The Games *will have been opened* by the flame.

EXERCISE 4

Place the verbs in parentheses in passive voice to complete the following sentences.

1. The first modern Olympic series (hold) _____ in Athens in 1896.
2. The first Olympic Village (build) _____ for the Games in 1932.
3. The Olympic flag (fly) _____ for the first time in 1920.
4. In the 1936 Olympics, the orchestra (lead) _____ by the composer Richard Strauss.
5. The Olympic Games (cancel) _____ in 1916 because of World War I.
6. The Summer Games (show) _____ on television for the first time in 1936.

GERUNDS

> **Strategy**
>
> A gerund, an infinitive, or a participle is a verbal, not a verb. Gerunds or infinitives can never take the place of a main verb in a sentence. When there is a verb missing in one of the test items, make sure you choose a verb and not a verbal.

The gerund is formed by adding *-ing* to the base form of a verb. The gerund is used as a noun. It can function as a subject, object, or object of a preposition.

***Running** is my favorite sport.* (subject)
He tried **running** faster. (object)
She was afraid of **losing.** (object of preposition)

When the gerund is the subject of the sentence, the verb is singular.

1. *Gerund after Noun + Prepositions.*

    The following are some nouns + prepositions that take gerunds:

choice of	excuse for	intention of
possibility of/for	reason for	method of/for

    *He has no intention of **giving up** now.*
    *There was no reason for **canceling** the race.*

2. *Gerund after Adjectives + Prepositions*

    The following are some adjectives + prepositions that take the gerund:

accustomed to	afraid of	capable of
fond of	good at	interested in
successful in	tired of	

    *She is accustomed to **training** for many hours.*
    *He is good at **running** the 200-meter race.*

3. **Gerunds after Verbs**

The following are some verbs that take the gerund:

admit	deny	postpone	resume
advise	discuss	practice	risk
anticipate	enjoy	quit	suggest
appreciate	excuse	recall	tolerate
avoid	finish	recommend	try
can't help	keep	regret	understand
consider	mind	resent	imagine
delay	miss	resist	

*He kept **running** until the end.*
*She enjoys **running** for competition.*

4. **Gerund after Verb + Preposition (Two-Word Verbs)**

The following are some two-word verbs that take the gerund:

approve of	give up	rely on
be better off	insist on	succeed in
call for	keep on	think about
confess to	look forward to	think of
count on	object to	worry about
depend on	put off	prevent from

*He succeeded in **winning** the race.*
*She did not give up **hoping**.*

5. **Gerund or Infinitive**

Some verbs can take either a gerund or an infinitive, with no difference in meaning. The following are verbs that can take either a gerund or infinitive:

advise	dread	mean	remember
agree	forget	neglect	start
allow	hate	permit	stop
attempt	intend	plan	study
begin	leave	prefer	try
continue	like	propose	
dislike	love	regret	

*I love **to watch** the track races.*
*I love **watching** the track races.*

INFINITIVES

The infinitive is formed by adding *to* to the base form of a verb. The infinitive can be used as a noun, an adjective, or an adverb.

To train is hard work. (noun)
She always has energy *to spend*. (adjective)
He ran *to win*. (adverb)

1. **Verbs That Take the Infinitive**

agree	decide	hope	prepare	threaten
appear	demand	intend	pretend	tend
arrange	deserve	learn	promise	try
ask	desire	manage	refuse	volunteer
attempt	expect	mean	regret	wait
beg	fail	need	seem	want
care	forget	offer	struggle	wish
claim	hire	order		

2. **Verb + Noun/Pronoun + Infinitive**

   The following verbs can be followed by a noun/pronoun and an infinitive:

advise	convince	force	order	teach
allow	challenge	hire	permit	tell
ask	encourage	instruct	persuade	want
cause	expect	invite	remind	warn
		need	require	

   He reminded me to keep calm.
   I taught him to swim.

3. **Adjective + Infinitive**

   The following are some adjectives that are followed by the infinitive:

anxious	easy	hard	ready
boring	good	pleased	strange
dangerous		prepared	usual
difficult			

   She was anxious to hear the results.
   It is hard to lose.

Exercise 5

Circle the letter of the word that correctly completes the sentence.

1. The authorities permitted women _____ in track and field events in the 1928 Winter Games.
   - (A) to take part
   - (B) taking part

2. Because of a lack of snow, three thousand Austrian soldiers were hired _____ in snow for the ski trails in 1964.
   - (A) bringing
   - (B) to bring

3. In ancient Greece it was agreed _____ wars for the Olympic Games.
   - (A) to stop
   - (B) stopping

4. Women were not allowed _____ in more than three events in 1932.
   - (A) participating
   - (B) to participate

5. The Roman Emperor Theodosius ordered the Games _____ in A.D. 394.
   - (A) stopping
   - (B) to stop

6. The two World Wars prevented the Olympics from _____ place.
   - (A) taking
   - (B) to take

ON THE TOEFL® TEST

In the Structure section, verb errors may involve the following:

1. *A verb may not agree with its subject.* A singular subject requires a singular verb and a plural subject requires a plural verb.

2. *A verb may be in the wrong tense.* The time words and the context will indicate the correct tense.

3. *A verb may be in the active form instead of the passive or vice versa.* If the subject does the action, the verb must be active; if the subject receives the action, the verb is passive.

4. *A verbal is not a verb.* A gerund or participle cannot be a main verb.

   Example: Electronic timing _____ for the first time in the 1912 Olympics in Sweden.

   (A) were used
   (B) was used
   (C) using
   (D) used

   The best answer is (B). (A) is incorrect because the subject is in gerund form and therefore requires a singular verb. (C) is incorrect because the *-ing* form is not a verb and a clause requires a verb. (D) is incorrect because the verb is active and a passive verb is needed.

In the Written Expression section, verb errors often involve the following:

1. *A main verb may be used instead of a participle or vice versa.* The main verb, for example *eat* or *ate,* may be used instead of *eaten,* or the main verb *is eating* instead of *eating.*

2. *The gerund may be used instead of the infinitive.* For example, *eating* instead of *to eat.*

3. *The wrong infinitive form may be used.* For example, *make* may be used instead of *to make.*

4. *The wrong form of the participle may be used.* The present participle may be used instead of the past participle or vice versa.

   Example In the 1931 Winter Olympics many competitors were
                                                               A
   prevented from to participate because of the economic
         B   C   D
   depression.

   The best choice is (C) because an infinitive cannot be used after a preposition. The gerund form *participating* must be used.

Exercises on Verbs

From the four words or phrases, choose the one that best completes the sentence.

1. The first systematic chart ever made of an ocean current _____ by Benjamin Franklin.
   (A) published
   (B) was published
   (C) publishing
   (D) has been published

2. Petroleum _____ on every continent and beneath every ocean.
   (A) is found
   (B) found
   (C) are found
   (D) find

3. Animals _____ on Earth for at least 700 million years.
   (A) living
   (B) lived
   (C) have lived
   (D) have been lived

4. During the Ice Age, glaciers _____ and retreated several times over large areas of the earth.
   (A) had been advanced
   (B) were advanced
   (C) have advanced
   (D) advanced

5. Some fish _____ distortions of electrical field through special receptors.
   (A) sense
   (B) are sensing
   (C) are sensed
   (D) senses

6. The widespread use of oil and gas to make chemicals _____ during the 1920s.
   (A) has begun
   (B) began
   (C) beginning
   (D) begun

CHAPTER 4 VERBS 47

From the four underlined words or phrases, identify the *one* that is not correct.

7. The American architect, Frank Lloyd Wright, <u>developed</u> a theory of
                                                    A
   architecture <u>stressed</u> the needs of the people <u>who</u> <u>used</u> it.
                   B   C   D

8. Pelicans <u>have</u> a long, straight bill with a <u>flexible</u> pouch <u>makes</u> of skin on
              A   B   C
   the <u>underside</u>.
          D

9. In some countries, octopuses and snails <u>are considered</u> <u>being</u> great
                                                A   B
   <u>delicacies</u> <u>to eat</u>.
       C   D

10. Many dyslexics <u>have</u> difficulty <u>to remembering</u> the <u>sequence</u> of letters in
                      A   B   C
    a word and in <u>distinguishing</u> right from left.
                         D

11. Men and women in the Peace Corps <u>work</u> with people in <u>developing</u>
                                       A   B
    countries to help them <u>improving</u> their <u>living</u> conditions.
                                C   D

12. Seahorses <u>spend</u> <u>much</u> of their time <u>clung</u> with their tails to <u>underwater</u>
                 A   B   C   D
    plants.

PREPOSITIONS

Introduction: Mount St. Helens

Mount St. Helens, a volcano in the state of Washington in the United States, erupted on May 18, 1980. Sixty-two people died due to the eruption. No one was surprised by the eruption on Mount St. Helens. Scientists had been predicting that an eruption was likely for almost two years before it happened.

In March 1980 a small eruption occurred and in April one side of the mountain started to swell and crack. The scientists issued warnings and asked people to clear the area. On May 18 the mountain exploded. Hot gases burst out, followed by hot ash, which ran down the mountain slopes burning everything in its path. Two cubic kilometers of earth was thrown 60,000 feet straight up into the atmosphere. Cities and towns were covered with powder. The ash from the volcano was found as far away as the Atlantic Ocean, on the other side of the continent.

The top of the mountain was blown away and about 600 square kilometers (230 miles) of land was destroyed, killing both animals and plants. Many thought it would take decades for the land to recover, but the return of life was remarkable. Today the slopes and valleys of Mount St. Helens once again have abundant wildlife.

EXERCISE 1

> **Prepositions are tested on the TOEFL® Test. Complete the sentences with the correct prepositions.**

1. Mount St. Helens erupted _____ May 18, 1980.
2. Scientists had predicted that an eruption was likely, so no one was surprised _____ it.
3. _____ April 1980 one side _____ the mountain started to swell.
4. The explosion of hot gases was followed _____ hot ash.
5. Cities were covered _____ ash from the mountain.
6. The ash _____ the mountain went as far as the Atlantic Ocean _____ the other side of the continent.

Exercise 2

> Look at the chart below showing natural disasters. Describe the disaster, including when it occurred, where it occurred, and what happened due to the disaster.

Disaster	Where	When	What Happened
Volcanic eruption	Krakatoa, Indonesia	August 27, 1883	36,000 people died
Potato famine	Ireland	1840s	1.5 million people died
Flood	Johnstown, Pennsylvania, U.S.	May 1889	2,200 people died
Earthquake	Tangshan, China	July 28, 1976	242,000 people died
Tidal wave	Bangladesh	1970	200,000 people died
Tornado	Ohio, U.S.	April 3, 1974	315 people died
Fire	Yellowstone Park, U.S.	1980	1.3 million acres burned

*A volcanic eruption **occurred in** Krakatoa **on** August 27, 1883. **Due to** the eruption, 36,000 people died.*

Grammar: Prepositions

Prepositions are not only used to show time, place, and agent but are also used in combination with verbs, adjectives, nouns, and in many common set expressions. All prepositions cannot be listed in this chapter, but it will present the important groups:

1. Verb + Preposition

    depend on   lead to

2. Adjective/Participle + Preposition

    surprised at   famous for

3. Noun + Preposition

    example of   possibility of

4. Other Combinations with Prepositions

    as a result of   in addition to

5. Prepositions of Time and Place

    on May 16   in Washington

6. Prepositions in Common Expressions

    at present   in general

VERB + PREPOSITION

account for	contribute to	insist on	plan on
believe in	depend on	lead to	rely on
belong to	detach from	obtain from	result in
confined to	fight for	overcome by	withdraw from

EXERCISE 3

Complete the sentences with the correct prepositions.

1. The destructive phenomena of Mount St. Helens were not confined _____ volcanic debris.

2. Valuable chemical products are obtained _____ volcanic substances, including gold and silver.

3. The 1989 San Francisco earthquake resulted _____ 59 deaths and massive property damage.

4. One growing season after another without rain quickly leads _____ starvation in many parts of the world.

5. Disease can sometimes be overcome _____ advances in modern medicine.

6. Since the Irish depended _____ their potato crop for food, the potato famine had devastating results.

7. Poor farming practices contributed _____ the dust bowl as much as weather conditions.

8. When there is famine in a country, the people must rely _____ the goodwill of other countries to provide them with the food they need.

ADJECTIVE/PARTICIPLE + PREPOSITION

accustomed to	different from	necessary for	responsible for
afraid of	expert at	opposed to	successful in
based on	free from	possible for	surprised at
compared to	famous for	related to	typical of

Exercise 4

Complete the sentences with the correct prepositions.

1. The 1980 Mount St. Helens eruption ranks low compared _____ other volcanic eruptions.

2. Some people think it is necessary _____ forest fires to happen occasionally so that new trees will grow.

3. Typical _____ American enterprise, a thriving cottage industry developed in marketing the ash from Mount St. Helens.

4. Volcanic ash in the atmosphere is responsible _____ brilliant red sunsets and sunrises.

5. The earth looks very different _____ the way it looked millions of years ago.

6. The type of gas ejected from a volcanic eruption is related _____ the volcano and the type of eruption.

7. Countries whose economy is entirely based _____ agriculture suffer most when a crop fails.

8. People were surprised _____ the amount of destruction the eruption of Mount St. Helens caused.

NOUN + PREPOSITION

cause of	equivalent of	influence on	result of
cost of	evidence of	need for	use of
danger of	example of	possibility of	solution to
effect on	increase in	reason for	supply of

Exercise 5

> Complete the sentences with the correct prepositions.

1. Mount St. Helens exploded in an eruption with the energy equivalent _____ 10 million tons of TNT.

2. With the ever-growing need _____ power, volcanoes and their by-products are of increasing value.

3. To the scientist, volcanoes provide first-hand evidence _____ the composition of the earth.

4. An example _____ an island that consists entirely of volcanic material is Iceland.

5. Iceland, Italy, New Zealand, and the state of California make practical use _____ volcanic steam.

6. The El Chichon eruption in Mexico had the greatest effect _____ the world's weather.

7. In recent years, the crater of Vesuvius has been sealed off to lessen the danger _____ another explosion.

8. Plague and famine can be results _____ social problems within a community.

OTHER COMBINATIONS WITH PREPOSITIONS

according to	in the process of
as a consequence of	in view of
as a result of	on account of
because of	on behalf of
by means of	on the basis of
in addition to	prior to
in spite of	with the exception of
in terms of	with the purpose of

CHAPTER 5   PREPOSITIONS   53

Exercise 6

> **Complete the sentences with the correct prepositions.**

1. According _____ some reports, the effect of the tsunami from Krakatoa was felt 11,000 miles away.

2. In addition _____ seismographs, tilt meters measure deformations of the surface before volcanic activity.

3. The loss in terms _____ individual trees after the Mount St. Helens eruptions came to six million.

4. Airplanes and trains were affected because _____ poor visibility after the eruption.

5. In view _____ their devastating results, much thought has been given to forecasting volcanic eruptions.

6. Thirty-five people died as a result _____ the Mount St. Helens eruption.

7. In spite _____ the death and destruction volcanoes cause, they benefit the land in many ways.

8. Prior _____ the eruption, a 300-foot bulge was observed on one side of Mount St. Helens.

PREPOSITIONS OF TIME AND PLACE

1. Prepositions of Time

at	time of day (at 8 a.m.)
	noon, night, midnight
in	parts of the day (in the morning/evening/afternoon)
	month (in July)
	season (in the fall)
	year (in 1980)
	decade (in the 1980s)
	century (in the nineteenth century)
on	days of the week (on Monday)
	dates (on March 20)
for/since	duration of time (for three days)
	point in time (since March 20)
from . . . to	beginning time . . . ending from (from 8 a.m. to 5 p.m.)

2. Prepositions of Place

at	address (at 200 Main Street)
on	street/road/avenue (on Kings Road)
	floor (on the second floor)
in	building (in the drugstore)
	city (in Los Angeles)
	state (in California)
	country (in Japan)
	continent (in Africa)
from . . . to	beginning point . . . ending point (from Alaska to California)

EXERCISE 7

Complete the sentences with the correct prepositions.

1. Mount St. Helens had last erupted _____ 1857.

2. Mount St. Helens exploded _____ about 8 a.m. Sunday.

3. The eruption was _____ May 18, 1980.

4. _____ the summer of 1816 the weather _____ the United States was affected by volcanic activity.

5. Mount St. Helens is _____ the state of Washington.

6. The volcano Paricutin _____ Mexico erupted _____ 1943.

7. Before the eruption, Mount St. Helens was in one of the most beautiful areas _____ North America.

8. Most houses _____ Reykjavik _____ Iceland are heated by natural steam.

9. Mount St. Helens started to be active _____ March 20 _____ May 18, 1980.

10. A chain of volcanoes runs _____ the East Indies _____ the Mediterranean.

PREPOSITIONS IN COMMON EXPRESSIONS

at times	by land/sea/air	in common	on fire
at present	by far	in general	on the other hand
at first/last	by chance	in existence	on the whole
at the moment	by accident	in the future/past	on purpose
	by day/night	in theory	on land

Exercise 8

Complete the sentences with the correct prepositions.

1. Volcanoes _____ land are best known, but those beneath the sea sometimes make headline news.
2. _____ times volcanoes have affected world weather.
3. _____ theory, volcanic eruptions are difficult to classify.
4. There are about 500 volcanoes _____ existence.
5. It looked as if the mountain were _____ fire.
6. Volcanic ash is destructive; _____ the other hand, it later produces a very fertile soil.
7. _____ general, a temperature of 100°C is reached at about 10,000 feet in the earth's crust.
8. Mount St. Helens was _____ far the most publicized eruption in recent times.

On the TOEFL® Test

Prepositions are tested in the Written Expression section of the exam. Check for these two types of errors with prepositions:

1. The wrong preposition is used.

    Example: Mount St. Helens, a volcano in Washington state
                                          A   B
    in the United States, erupted in May 18, 1980.
          C   D

    The correct answer is (C); the preposition *on* must be used before a date (*in* is used before a month without a date).

    Example: After the eruption of Mount St. Helens in 1980, the height of
                        A   B   C
    the mountain was reduced of 400 meters.
                           D

    The correct answer is (D); the preposition *by* should be used after the verb "reduce" in this sentence.

2. A preposition may be omitted or a preposition may be used when it is not necessary.

Example: Despite of its isolation in the Sunda Strait between Java and
              A   B   C
Sumatra, over 36,000 people died in the tidal waves follow-
                                        D
ing the explosion of Krakatoa.

The correct answer is (A); the preposition *of* should not be used in this phrase (*of* is used in the phrase *in spite of,* but *despite,* which has the same meaning, does not take a preposition).

Example: According experts 60,000 cubic feet of earth was thrown
             A   B
into the air in the explosion of Mount St. Helens.
    C   D

The best answer is (A); the preposition *to* has been omitted from the phrase *according to.*

Exercises on Prepositions

> **Identify** one of the underlined words or phrases (A), (B), (C), or (D) that should be rewritten or corrected.

1. The rocky island of Alcatraz in San Francisco Bay was discovered by the
                                  A   B
Spanish in 1769 and named by its large pelican colony.
      C   D

2. Bacteria are responsible of many of the textures and flavors in our food
              A   B   C
and are particularly important in milk products.
                    D

3. Art Nouveau, a style that was in fashion in the 1890s, was based of long
                           A   B   C
curving lines inspired by climbing plants.
            D

4. The brain is made up of billions of neurons that differ with each other
               A   B   C
greatly in size and shape.
      D

5. Wood, the hardened material from which trees are composed, is
                   A   B
made up of millions of tiny tubes of fibers packed together.
     C   D

CHAPTER 5   PREPOSITIONS   57

6. Animals that <u>live in areas</u> that are <u>covered in</u> snow <u>in winter</u> change the
                        A   B   C
   color of their coat <u>according</u> the seasons.
                                D

7. The <u>need for vitamins</u> <u>of our diet</u> was <u>discovered by</u> the Dutch doctor
               A   B   C
   Christiaan Eijkman <u>in 1896</u>.
                          D

8. Many of the <u>satellites</u> <u>of space</u> carry telescopes and other instruments
                 A   B
   <u>used in astronomy</u> to <u>look at the stars</u>.
           C   D

9. Homes that have cable television <u>get their programs</u>
                                  A
   <u>from a local television station</u> <u>through a cable</u> <u>connected with</u> the set.
            B   C   D

10. Henry David Thoreau stressed <u>the importance in</u> individuality and
                                      A
    <u>of living</u> <u>in harmony</u> <u>with</u> nature.
       B   C   D

11. The hormone insulin <u>controls by</u> <u>the amount of sugar</u> <u>in the blood</u>,
                     A   B   C
    which <u>provides energy</u> for the body.
            D

12. Frogs get <u>much of their</u> oxygen <u>by means blood</u> capillaries <u>in the surface</u>
              A   B   C
    <u>of the skin</u>.
      D

CHAPTER 6 ARTICLES

Introduction: Islands

The world's ten largest islands (drawn to scale)

Island	Ocean	Island	Ocean
1. Greenland	Arctic	6. Sumatra	Indian
2. New Guinea	Pacific	7. Honshu	Pacific
3. Borneo	Pacific	8. Great Britain	Atlantic
4. Madagascar	Indian	9. Victoria	Arctic
5. Baffin Island	Arctic	10. Ellesmere	Arctic

Some islands were originally parts of continents. These islands were separated from the mainland as a result of a rise in sea level. For example, Great Britain was connected to the mainland of Europe about 11,000 years ago. As the climate got warmer, ice melted and the sea level rose. As a result, water covered the land that had connected Great Britain to the mainland.

Other islands rise from the ocean. Some are volcanoes, such as the islands of Hawaii and the islands of Japan. Some volcanic islands are millions of years old, but new islands are forming all the time. For example, Iceland was formed millions of years ago by a volcano. In 1963, a volcano started to form a new island called Surtsey near Iceland.

Islands differ greatly in size. Greenland is the largest island in the world. The difference between an island and a continent is based on size. Because Australia is three times the size of Greenland, geographers classify Australia as a continent.

EXERCISE 1

Articles are tested on the TOEFL® Test. Complete the sentences with the name of the country or island.

1. Honshu is the biggest island in _____.
2. _____ is the biggest island in the world.
3. According to geographers, _____ is not an island but a continent.
4. About 11,000 years ago _____ was connected to Europe.
5. _____ was formed by a volcano millions of years ago.
6. _____ is a new island formed in 1963.

Exercise 2

Complete the sentences below with information from the chart.

1. Greenland is the largest island. It is in the _____ Ocean.
2. _____ is the second largest island. It is in the _____ Ocean.
3. _____ is _____ _____ largest island. It is in _____ _____ Ocean.
4. _____ is _____ _____ largest island. It is in _____ _____ Ocean.
5. _____ is _____ fifth largest island. It is in _____ _____ Ocean.
6. _____ is _____ _____ largest island. It is in _____ _____ Ocean.

Grammar: Articles

THE INDEFINITE ARTICLE *A* OR *AN*

Strategy

Avoid confusion between *a* and *an*. Remember, *an* is used before a vowel sound.

The indefinite article *a* or *an* is used:

1. Before singular count nouns to mean *one*. It is not used before non-count nouns.

   Australia is **a** continent.

2. *An* is used before a word that begins with a vowel sound (a, e, i, o, u). When words begin with "h" or "u," either *a* or *an* can be used depending on the sound:

an uncle	**a** home
a university	**an** hour
a union	**an** honor

CHAPTER 6 ARTICLES 61

3. In a general statement:

   An island is a body of land surrounded by water.

4. To introduce a subject that has not been mentioned before:

   I saw **a** snake.

5. With certain numerical expressions:

a dozen	**a** couple	**a** hundred	**a** third	**a** half
a great many	**a** great deal	**a** lot of	*fifty miles **an** hour	*$10 **a** day

   * In this case *a/an* is a replacement for *per*.

6. With names of professions:

   He is **an** engineer.   She is **a** biologist.

EXERCISE 3

> Circle *a* or *an* in the following sentences. Write "C" on the left if the sentence is correct. Write "NC" if the sentence is not correct. Correct the error.

_____ 1. Indonesia is a country made up of thousands of islands.

_____ 2. Greenland is an big island with a permanent ice cap covering it.

_____ 3. The Bahamas, which consist of 700 islands, have a superb climate.

_____ 4. Robinson Crusoe is a character in a book by Daniel Defoe.

_____ 5. Robinson Crusoe spent twenty years with his friend Man Friday on a uninhabited island.

_____ 6. New Guinea is a country where there are a 700 languages.

_____ 7. Etna is an active volcano on the island of Sicily.

_____ 8. On the island of Borneo, there is a snake that can fly or leap up to 20 meters.

_____ 9. The plants and an animals that live on an island may develop to be quite different.

THE DEFINITE ARTICLE *THE*

> **Strategy**
>
> Do not confuse *a/an* with *the*. Learn the rules for the use of *a/an and the*. The articles are often used one in place of the other on the exam.

The definite article *the* can be used before any noun, singular, plural, count, and noncount, when the noun is specific.

The island
The islands
The water

The definite article is used:

1. When there is only *one* of the thing mentioned:

   The sun is shining.
   The sky is blue.

2. When it is clear to both the speaker and the listener which thing or person is referred to:

   Could you open the door please? (Both the speaker and the listener know which door it is.)

3. Before a noun mentioned for the second time:

   A bird flew into the classroom.
   The bird sat on my desk.

4. Before superlative adjectives:

   The biggest island is Greenland.
   The most beautiful coral island is very small.

5. Before names of musical instruments:

   He plays the piano.

6. Before a singular noun representative of a class of things (names of animals, plants, inventions, and parts of the body):

   The dodo is an extinct bird.
   The Rafflesia is the world's largest flower.
   Alexander Graham Bell invented the telephone.
   He hit me on the head.

CHAPTER 6 ARTICLES 63

> **Strategy**
>
> Remember the uses of the definite article. It may be omitted when it should not be on the exam.

7. Before decades and centuries:

   the 1800s   *the* twenties   *the* twentieth century

8. Before expressions of time and place:

the morning	*the* future
the afternoon	*the* present
the evening	*the* past

the north	*the* front
the south	*the* back
the east	*the* middle
the west	*the* top
	the bottom

9. Before ordinal numbers (the definite article is not used with cardinal numbers):

Ordinal numbers:	Cardinal numbers:
The first	One
The second day	Day two
The sixth lesson	Lesson six

10. When speaking about a specific noun:

    Coffee originated in Ethiopia. (general)
    The coffee I had this morning was Brazilian. (specific)

11. Before names of countries, states, cities, universities, colleges, and schools that contain the word "of," and before countries that have a plural name or have an adjective in the name, except for Great Britain:

    The United States of America
    The state of Florida
    The city of Boston
    The University of Texas
    But: *Boston University*
    The Netherlands
    The Philippines

12. Before names of oceans, rivers, seas, gulfs, and plural names of mountains, islands, and lakes (no article is used with singular mountains, islands, and lakes):

    The Pacific Ocean   *The* Mississippi River
    The Gulf of Mexico   *The* Black Sea
    The Appalachian Mountains   Mount Washington
    The Hawaiian islands   Manhattan Island
    The Great Lakes   Lake Michigan

13. Before geographic areas, but not before names of continents:

    The Middle East   *Asia*
    The Orient   *Europe*

14. Before the names of fields of study when they contain the word *of*:

    The History of the United States   History
    The Literature of the Sixties   Biology

15. Before the names of wars (not including the World Wars):

    The War of Independence   *The* Civil War
    World War II   *The* Second World War

16. Before the names of ships, planes, trains, and people's family names (the definite article is not used with the names of people and names of magazines):

    The Browns   Robert Brown
    The Mayflower   Time *Magazine*
    The Orient Express

Exercise 4

Fill in the blanks with the correct article *a*, *an*, *the*, or *ø*.

1. Islands make up __the__ entire land area of some countries, including _____ Japan and __the__ Philippines.

2. __The__ Florida Keys are coastal islands built on coral reefs.

3. _____ Mackinac Island in _____ Lake Michigan is __a__ lake island.

4. __The__ city of Montreal, in _____ Canada, is built on __a__ large river island.

5. __The__ Aleutian Islands, part of _____ Alaska, are __a__ string of coastal islands that were built by _____ volcanoes.

CHAPTER 6 ARTICLES 65

6. On __the__ big island of Hawaii is one of __the__ world's greatest volcanoes, _____ Mauna Loa.
7. Kilauea is __the__ most active volcano in __the__ state of _____ Hawaii.
8. The early settlers of __the__ Pacific Islands, __the__ Polynesians, always carried _____ coconuts with them in their canoes.
9. In _____ Indonesia is __a__ huge lizard, __the__ Komodo Dragon, that eats deer and attacks people.
10. __The__ dodo, a giant bird now extinct, lived on __the__ island of Mauritius, in __the__ Indian Ocean.

On the TOEFL® Test

Articles are tested in the Written Expression section of the exam. Check for these three types of errors with articles:

1. The article may be used when it is not necessary, or not used when it is necessary.

    Example: Pelican Island in Florida and Oregon Islands in Oregon are
                            A   B   C
    wildlife refuges.
           D

    The best answer is (C); the definite article *the* should not be omitted from the name of a plural group of islands.

    Example: The most coral islands develop from reefs that grow up
                   A   B   C
    around volcanic islands.
            D

    The best answer is (A). This is not a superlative form; therefore the article is not necessary.

2. *An* is used instead of *a* or vice versa. Also *a* or *an* may be used instead of *the* or vice versa.

    Example: A broad expanse of sea with a large number of islands is
                 A   B   C
    called a archipelago.
         D

    The best answer is (D). *An* must be used before a noun beginning with a vowel sound.

    Example: When the island of Surtsey was eighteen months old a first
                A   B   C
    leafy green plant appeared.
        D

    The best answer is (C). The definite article *the* must be used with an ordinal number.

3. Another word like a possessive adjective may be used instead of the article or vice versa.

Example: The new island of Surtsey is its ideal natural laboratory for scientists.
A   B   C
D

The best answer is (C). The indefinite article *an* meaning "one" must be used.

Example: Coral reefs are limestone formations composed of tiny sea organisms and the remains.
A   B
C   D

The best answer is (D). The possessive adjective *their* must replace the definite article *the* to show its reference to sea organisms.

Exercises on Articles

> From the four underlined words or phrases (A), (B), (C), or (D), identify the one that is not correct.

1. The watt is named after James Watt, the British engineer who developed the steam engine in 1760s.
   A   B
          C   D

2. Methane is a odorless burning gas and is the main ingredient of natural gas.
   A   B   C
   D

3. The alcohol acts as a narcotic on the nervous system and the brain.
   A   B   C   D

4. Zachary Taylor was first president to be elected from a state west of the Mississippi River.
                  A   B   C
   D

5. Barnacles, which are related to lobsters, shrimp, and crabs, make strongest glue.
   A   B   C
   D

6. In the 1860s Louis Pasteur discovered that bacteria in air caused the perishable food to go bad.
      A   B
      C   D

CHAPTER 6 ARTICLES 67

7. Land covers almost third of the earth's surface, of which two-thirds is
   —A—   —B—   —C—   —D—
   too cold or too dry for farming.

8. "Old Faithful" in the Yellowstone National Park is probably the world's
                —A— —————B—————   —————C—————
   most famous geyser.
   ———D———

9. Thermographs are special pictures that show the variation in heat
   ——A——   ————B————   —C—
   emitted by different areas of body.
                              —D—

10. The world's fastest animal is cheetah, but if birds are included,
    ————A————   —B—
    the fastest of all animals is the spine-tailed swift.
    ————C————   ———————D———————

11. The most of the energy used in our homes and factories is generated
    ————A———— ——B——
    from coal, oil, and natural gas.
         —C— —D—

12. Soybeans were first grown in the Orient and brought to the Western
    ———A———   ————B————   ————C————
    world during the World War Two.
                 ————————D————————

CHAPTER 7

NOUN CLAUSES

Introduction: Michael Faraday

During the last 400 years, most scientists have relied on mathematics in their development of their inventions or discoveries. However, one great British scientist, Michael Faraday, did not make use of mathematics. Faraday, the son of a poor blacksmith, was born in London in 1791 and had no education beyond reading and writing.

In 1812 Faraday was hired as a bottle washer by the great chemist Humphry Davy. Later, Faraday became a greater scientist than Davy, making the last years of Davy's life embittered with jealousy.

Faraday made the first electric motor in 1821, a device that used electricity to produce movement. Then Faraday became interested in the relationship between electricity and magnetism. In 1831 he discovered that when a magnet is moved near a wire, electricity flows in the wire. With this discovery he produced a machine for making electricity called a dynamo. Faraday then went on to show how electricity affects chemical substances.

Because Faraday believed that money should be given to the poor, when he grew old, he was destitute. However, Queen Victoria rewarded him for his discoveries by giving him a stipend and a house. He died in 1867.

EXERCISE 1

Noun clauses are tested on the TOEFL® Test. Complete the blanks in the following sentences with *that* and *how*.

1. Humphry Davy was jealous _____that_____ Faraday became a greater scientist than he.
2. Faraday discovered _____that_____ when a magnet is moved near a wire it produces electricity.
3. Faraday showed _____how_____ electricity affects chemical substances.
4. Faraday showed _____how_____ great scientific discoveries could be made without the use of mathematics.

5. Faraday believed __that__ money should be given to the poor.
6. Faraday's invention meant __that__ homes could be heated by electric power and lit by electric light.

Exercise 2

> **Choose the correct noun clause to complete the sentence.**

1. Faraday discovered _____.
   - (A) that a magnet creates electricity in a wire
   - (B) what electricity is

2. Faraday showed _____.
   - (A) why electricity does not affect chemicals
   - (B) how electricity affects chemical substances

3. It was obvious _____.
   - (A) why Humphry Davy was jealous of Faraday
   - (B) how Humphry Davy was jealous of Faraday

4. Faraday believed _____.
   - (A) what everybody told him
   - (B) that money was not important

5. It can be seen _____.
   - (A) how mathematics is important to scientific discovery
   - (B) that mathematics is not necessarily important in scientific discovery

Grammar: Noun Clauses

A noun clause is a subordinate clause. A noun clause has a subject and a verb, and can be used like a noun, either as a subject or an object.

1. As Subject

   <u>His discovery</u> was important.
       Noun

   His discovery is a noun. It is the subject of the sentence.

   <u>What he discovered</u> was important.
       Noun clause

   What he discovered is a noun clause. It is the subject of the sentence. It has a subject *he* and a verb *discovered*.

2. *As Object*

People believed <u>his discovery</u>.
                    Noun

His discovery is a noun. It is the object of the verb *believed*.

People believed <u>what he discovered</u>.
                    Noun clause

What he discovered is a noun clause. It is the object of the verb *believed*.

Noun clauses are introduced by the following words:

when	who/whom	whether	that
where	what	if	
why	which		
how	whose		

NOUN CLAUSES BEGINNING WITH A QUESTION WORD

Question words such as *when, where, why, how, who/whom, what, which,* and *whose* can introduce a noun clause.

	Question	Noun Clause
1.	What did he discover?	I don't know *what he discovered*.
2.	When did he discover it?	I'm not sure *when he discovered it*.
3.	Where did he discover it?	It is not known *where he discovered it*.
4.	How did he discover it?	I'm not certain *how he discovered it*.
5.	Who is Faraday?	I don't know *who he is*.
6.	Whose discovery is that?	It is not certain *whose discovery that is*.
7.	What did he discover?	*What he discovered* is not certain. (*What he discovered* is the subject of the sentence.)

CHAPTER 7   NOUN CLAUSES   71

> **Strategy**
>
> Do not use question word order in a noun clause. The subject comes before the verb in a noun clause.

EXERCISE 3

> **Which of the following sentences do not have correct word order in the noun clause? Write "C" for correct or "NC" for not correct.**

_____ 1. It is amazing what discovered Faraday in the field of science without the use of mathematics.

___C___ 2. Early scientists did not know how a strong, steady electrical current could be produced.

___C___ 3. How Faraday did his experiments without the use of mathematics is not known.

_____ 4. In the early 1800s it was unknown what was the electric current.

_____ 5. People have known what are the effects of electricity since ancient times.

___C___ 6. Before Faraday's experiments, people were unsure what the connection between electricity and magnetism was.

NOUN CLAUSES BEGINNING WITH *WHETHER* OR *IF*

When a yes/no question is changed to a noun clause, *whether* or *if* is used to introduce the clause.

Question	Noun Clause
Will it work?	He wonders *whether it will work*.
	He wonders *if it will work*.
Did they believe him?	I don't know *whether they believed him*.
	I don't know *if they believed him*.

NOUN CLAUSES BEGINNING WITH *THAT*

For a statement of a fact or an idea, the word *that* is used to introduce the noun clause.

	Statement	Noun Clause
1.	The world is round.	We know *that the world is round*. (*That the world is round* is the object of the verb *know*.)
2.	The world is round.	We know *the world is round*. (The word *that* is frequently omitted in spoken English.)
3.	The world is round.	*That the world is round* is a fact. (*That the world is round* is the subject of the sentence. The word *that* cannot be omitted when it introduces a noun clause that is the subject of a sentence.)

Strategy

A noun clause must have a subject and a verb. Look for a subject and a verb when the noun clause is the object or the subject of a sentence.

EXERCISE 4

Circle the letter of the correct noun clause that completes the sentence.

1. Faraday argued that _____.
   - (A) electricity in a wire magnetic effect
   - (B) electricity in a wire by magnetic effect
   - (C) electricity in a wire produced a magnetic effect
   - (D) a magnetic effect produced by electricity in a wire

2. It is a fact that _____ form of energy.
   - (A) electricity is the most useful
   - (B) electricity the most useful
   - (C) the most useful in electricity
   - (D) electricity being the most useful

3. _____ over long distances is a fact.
   (A) That electricity can be transmitted
   (B) That electricity transmitting
   (C) That electricity
   (D) That can be transmitted

4. Today it is known that _____ magnetism.
   (A) electricity relating to
   (B) electricity is related to
   (C) relating to electricity
   (D) as electricity to

5. _____ in science was important for Faraday.
   (A) Children that were interested
   (B) That children interested
   (C) That children should be interested
   (D) That interested children

6. After listening to Humphry Davy, Faraday realized that _____.
   (A) wanting to be a scientist
   (B) being a scientist
   (C) wanted to be a scientist
   (D) he wanted to be a scientist

On the TOEFL® Test

In a typical noun clause error, a part of the noun clause is missing from the stem. The missing part may be the introductory word, the subject, the verb, or even the whole noun clause.

It is important to:

1. Look for the correct word order in the distractors.
2. See if the noun clause has a subject and a verb.
3. Find the correct introductory word for the noun clause.

   Example: _____ was flat was believed by most people in the fifteenth century.
   (A) The Earth
   (B) That the Earth
   (C) As the Earth
   (D) Whether the Earth

   The best answer is (B). (A) is not correct because there are two verbs—*was* and *was believed*—and only one subject. (C) is incorrect because the introductory word does not make sense in the sentence. (D) is incorrect because it does not have a subject.

   Example: Many scientists have shown _____ can be used for an ever-increasing number of tasks.
   (A) that lasers how
   (B) lasers how
   (C) how lasers
   (D) that what lasers

   The best answer is (C).

Exercises on Noun Clauses

From the four words or phrases (A), (B), (C), or (D), choose the *one* that best completes the sentence.

1. Astronomers studied the 1987 Supernova to learn _____ when a star explodes.
   - (A) what happens
   - (B) that happens
   - (C) that is happen
   - (D) what does happen

2. Despite recent attempts to prove _____ did indeed reach the North Pole in 1909, the evidence still remains questionable.
   - (A) what Robert Peary
   - (B) that Robert Peary
   - (C) Robert Peary, who
   - (D) Robert Peary was

3. Around 1789, Antoine Lavoisier was the first person to demonstrate _____ all kinds of burning involve the addition of oxygen.
   - (A) if
   - (B) what
   - (C) that
   - (D) so that

4. Where _____ is the commonest form of color-blindness.
   - (A) are the red and green not easily distinguished
   - (B) they are not easily distinguished red and green
   - (C) are not easily distinguished red and green
   - (D) red and green are not easily distinguished

5. It has been estimated _____ milligram of skin scales have over half a million bacteria.
   - (A) that a
   - (B) how a
   - (C) a
   - (D) to be a

6. It is only in the last 200 years _____ have begun climbing mountains.
   - (A) because people
   - (B) that people
   - (C) people
   - (D) as people

7. _____ of smell might, without our realizing it, affect who we choose as friends has been suggested.
   - (A) That our sense
   - (B) Sense
   - (C) For our sense
   - (D) Because our sense

8. From the existence of radio waves, most scientists were convinced _____ really happened.
   - (A) the Big Bang was
   - (B) it was the Big Bang
   - (C) how the Big Bang
   - (D) that the Big Bang

9. Samples of rock showed _____ 4600 million years old.
   (A) that the moon is
   (B) how is the moon
   (C) when is the moon
   (D) to be the moon

10. _____ was lowered to the sea bed in a glass container to make observations is debated.
    (A) Alexander the Great who
    (B) Whether Alexander the Great
    (C) Alexander the Great
    (D) What Alexander the Great

11. _____ so incredible is that it can grow 385 miles of roots in four months, or about 3 miles in a day.
    (A) That makes the rye plant
    (B) What makes the rye plant
    (C) The rye plant
    (D) The rye plant which was

12. Science fiction writers believe _____ in the future, with new material and greater knowledge, their vision will become reality.
    (A) that they
    (B) they
    (C) that
    (D) they will

ADJECTIVE CLAUSES

Introduction: American Indian Smoke Signals

The smoke signals used by American Indians did not convey the complex messages seen in Hollywood movies. Smoke signals were in fact used among the seminomadic tribes of the Great Plains. However, their content was limited to a few simple messages whose meaning had been agreed upon in advance. For example, Piman warriors in Arizona who had just finished a successful raid might send up a column of smoke, and the village would reply with two columns of smoke. Smoke signals were most commonly used to broadcast news of victory in battle, or to warn of sickness in a camp or dangers such as approaching enemies.

Fires fed with damp grass or boughs of evergreen sent up the one or two simple, unbroken columns of smoke needed to send a message. The place that the signal came from—whether on a hill or in a valley—conveyed most of the meaning. When Apaches out hunting spotted another group of Indians in the distance, they lit a fire conspicuously to the right of their own party that meant, "Who are you?" If the others were friends, they would then use a prearranged reply.

EXERCISE 1

Adjective clauses are tested on the TOEFL® Test. Complete the sentences with the relative pronouns *which, who, whose*.

1. The smoke signals ____which____ the American Indians used did not convey complex messages.

2. The signals contained simple messages ____whose____ meaning had been agreed upon in advance.

3. A warrior ____who____ had finished a successful raid might send a simple column of smoke to his village.

4. They made fires ____which____ were fed with damp grass.

5. It was the place the signal came from ____which____ conveyed most of the message.

6. When one group spotted another group of Indians, they lit a fire to their right ____which____ meant, "Who are you?"

Exercise 2

> **Choose the correct relative pronoun in parentheses to complete the sentence.**

1. The seminomadic tribes of the Great Plains used smoke signals (which/who) were simple.

2. A signal (whose/which) conveyed victory in battle was agreed upon in advance.

3. The Hollywood movies (which/whom) we watch do not give a true picture of the Indians.

4. A party would send a column of smoke (which/whom) the other understood.

5. Drumbeats (whose/which) are used by tribes in Africa can give more complex signals.

6. A warrior (who/which) saw an enemy approaching might send a smoke signal.

Grammar: Adjective Clauses

An adjective clause contains a subject and a verb. An adjective clause is a subordinate or dependent clause, it must be connected to a main or independent clause. An adjective clause modifies a noun. Adjective clauses begin with a relative pronoun such as *who, whom, whose, which, that,* or a relative adverb such as *when* or *where.*

IDENTIFYING ADJECTIVE CLAUSES

Clause Marker	Use	Example
who	People (subject)	The tribes *who* lived in the Great Plains used smoke signals.
whom	People (object)	The woman *whom* we met was called Lightning Cloud.
whose	People/things (possessive)	He sent a message *whose* meaning we had agreed upon in advance.
which	Things (subject/object)	That is a tribe *which* interests me. (subject)
		The drumbeats *which* we heard sent a message. (object)
that	People/things (subject/object)	The Apache is a tribe *that* I will research. (object)
		The smoke *that* you see is from the hills. (subject)
where	Place (adverb)	That is the valley *where* the tribe lived.
when	Time (adverb)	That is the day *when* we get the signal.

Strategy

Check for the correct clause marker and a subject and verb in an adjective clause.

EXERCISE 3

Underline the adjective clauses in the following sentences.

1. Sacagawea, who was a Shoshoni Indian, guided Lewis and Clark to the Columbia River.

2. The giant redwood trees that grow in California are named after Sequoyah, who created an alphabet for the Indian people.

3. Sequoyah became a teacher and moved to Oklahoma where he continued to teach the alphabet.

4. The Shoshoni were a group of Indians who lived in the western plains of Wyoming, Utah, Nevada, and Idaho.

5. Each group of Shoshoni was known to the others by the type of food that was plentiful in its particular region.

6. The Mossi people of West Africa use talking drums as a means of preserving their history, which has been handed down by generations.

> **Strategy**
>
> Remember that sometimes the relative pronoun may be omitted from an adjective clause. The relative pronouns *which, that, who,* and *whom* can be omitted when they are the object of the adjective clause.

OMISSION OF THE RELATIVE PRONOUN

When the relative pronoun is the subject of the adjective clause, it cannot be omitted.

*The man **who** played the drum was from West Africa.* (subject)

If the relative pronoun is the object of the adjective clause, it can be omitted.

*The man **whom** I saw was a Native American.* (object)
The man I saw was a Native American.

*The drumbeat **that** I heard was a signal.* (object)
The drumbeat I heard was a signal.

The relative pronouns *whose, where,* and *whereby* cannot be omitted.

*Sequoyah, **whose** alphabet for the Indian people consisted of 85 characters, was acclaimed a genius by his people. (Whose cannot be omitted.)*

*That was the area **where** the tribe lived. (Where cannot be omitted.)*

*Sequoyah devised an alphabet **whereby** all the different tribes could read a common language. (Whereby cannot be omitted.)*

> **Strategy**
> Look for prepositions that come before adjective clauses.

PREPOSITIONS THAT COME BEFORE ADJECTIVE CLAUSES

Sometimes an adjective clause is used with a preposition.

> *There are a number of ways **by which** a message can be sent.*

In spoken English the preposition usually goes at the end of the clause, but in formal written English it goes at the beginning of the clause.

> *Formal: That was the man **to whom** I was referring.*
> *Informal: That was the man **whom** I was referring **to**.*

EXERCISE 4

> **Circle the number of the sentence where the relative pronoun/adverb or a preposition is missing.**

1. Lewis and Clark went to South Dakota, where they spent a bitter winter among the Mandan tribe.
2. It is countries such as Ghana, Dahoney, and Nigeria the use of talking drums is mostly highly developed.
3. The most celebrated talking drummers of West Africa are the Yorubas whose principal instrument is known as a dondon.
4. Talking drums, play a central role in African cultural and social life, have many uses besides the sending of long-distance messages.
5. There are a number of colors which the Pueblo Indians of America identified direction.
6. Drumbeats which the actual words of their tribal language is communicated is a traditional form of communication in Africa.

REDUCED ADJECTIVE CLAUSES

> **Strategy**
>
> Look for a reduced adjective clause, also called an adjective phrase. An adjective phrase does not contain a subject and a verb.

Adjective clauses can be reduced to phrases. An adjective phrase modifies a noun. An adjective phrase does not contain a subject and a verb.

> *Adjective Clause: The man who is drumming is African.*
> *Adjective Phrase: The man drumming is African.*

Only adjectives that have a subject pronoun, *who, which,* or *that,* can be reduced.

> *Clause: The man who is playing the drums is well-known.*
> *Phrase: The man playing the drums is well-known.*

> *Clause: The man (whom) I met was well-known.*
> *Phrase: not possible*

There are two ways to reduce an adjective phrase.

1. The subject pronoun and the *be* form of the verb are omitted.

   > *Clause: The man who is playing is my friend.*
   > *Phrase: The man playing is my friend.*

   > *Clause: The signals which are given are simple.*
   > *Phrase: The signals given are simple.*

   > *Clause: The tones that are in the language are important.*
   > *Phrase: The tones in the language are important.*

2. When there is no form of *be* in the adjective clause, you can omit the subject pronoun and change the verb to the *-ing* form.

   > *Clause: The Cherokee Indians have an alphabet that consists of eighty-five characters.*
   > *Phrase: The Cherokee Indians have an alphabet consisting of eighty-five characters.*

   > *Clause: Anyone who wants to get the news can listen to the message.*
   > *Phrase: Anyone wanting to get the news can listen to the message.*

   Adjective phrases are usually separated by commas, as in adjective clauses.

   > *Clause: Sequoyah, who was the inventor of an Indian alphabet, was a Cherokee Indian.*
   > *Phrase: Sequoyah, the inventor of an Indian alphabet, was a Cherokee Indian.*

Exercise 5

> Where possible, reduce the adjective clauses to phrases.

1. Sequoyah, who was the son of an Indian mother and a European father, was born in Tennessee.

2. Sequoyah, who was first a hunter, became a trader after a hunting accident.

3. Sequoyah, who had no education, believed that reading and writing were important.

4. Sequoyah, who worked on the alphabet for twelve years, finally completed it in 1823.

5. His alphabet, which consists of eighty-five sounds, was an important invention for his people.

6. A Cherokee newspaper whose columns had news both in English and Cherokee was soon published.

7. Thousands of Cherokees who did not know how to read or write started to write using the new alphabet.

On the TOEFL® Test

Adjective clauses are tested in the Structure section of the exam. In the item, certain or all parts of an adjective clause may be missing. It is important to remember what an adjective clause is and what an adjective phrase is; that is, if a subject and verb are necessary or not.

Example: Pythons live in rugged tropical areas _____ heavy rainfall and forests.

(A) they have
(B) that have
(C) where the
(D) have

The best answer is (B). (C) is incorrect because *where* is the incorrect connector and the clause does not have a verb. (A) is incorrect because there is no connector joining the first and second clause. (D) is incorrect because there is no connector between the verb *have* and the rest of the sentence.

Reduced adjective clauses are also tested in the Structure section. Again, part or all of the phrase may be missing from the stem.

Example: In 1880, George Eastman, _____ dry-plate manufacturer, introduced the Kodak box camera.

(A) who an American
(B) he was an American
(C) an American
(D) was an American

The best choice is (C); (A) is incorrect because there is no verb in the relative clause. (B) does not have a connector to join the clause to the rest of the sentence. (D) is not correct because it contains a verb and a phrase cannot have a verb.

Exercises on Adjective Clauses

From the four words or phrases (A), (B), (C), or (D), choose the *one* that best completes the sentence.

1. The thyroid gland, _____, is located in the neck.
   (A) where the hormone thyroxine is produced
   (B) where produced is the hormone thyroxine
   (C) the hormone thyroxine is produced there
   (D) at which is produced the hormone thyroxine

2. Dragonflies feed on a large variety of insects _____ catch in flight.
   (A) in which they
   (B) which they
   (C) there are to
   (D) there are a

3. According to legend, Betsy Ross was the woman _____ the first American stars and stripes flag.
   (A) whom she made
   (B) made
   (C) who made
   (D) and she made

4. Pumpkin seeds, _____ protein and iron, are a popular snack.
   (A) that
   (B) provide
   (C) which
   (D) which provide

5. The spinal cord is a long, thick bundle of nerves _____ from the brain to the lower part of the back.
   (A) that runs
   (B) is running
   (C) it runs
   (D) whom it runs

6. George Pullman introduced a dining car _____ its own kitchen in 1868.

   (A) it had
   (B) that had
   (C) that it had
   (D) having

7. In 1898, _____ pharmacologist, John H. Abel, isolated the hormone adrenaline.

   (A) an American who
   (B) who, an American
   (C) an American
   (D) he was an American

8. Nitrogen gas, _____ up about 78 percent of our atmosphere, is constantly being used by plants and animals.

   (A) which it makes
   (B) it makes
   (C) makes
   (D) which makes

9. Paper is made from cellulose fibers, _____ in all cells.

   (A) are
   (B) which are
   (C) they are
   (D) which they are

10. The pepper plant bears a small, green berry _____ red as it ripens.

    (A) which turns
    (B) turns
    (C) it turns
    (D) that it turns

11. Quinine, _____ once used to cure malaria, was taken from the bark of a South American tree, the cinchona.

    (A) it is a famous drug
    (B) is a famous drug
    (C) a famous drug
    (D) is a famous drug whose

12. Billie Holiday, _____ unique singing style made her famous, was also known as Lady Day.

    (A) she is a
    (B) whom
    (C) who
    (D) whose

CHAPTER 9
ADVERB CLAUSES

Introduction: Distant Galaxies

The development of the radio telescope has led to two of the most important discoveries in modern astronomy: the identification of the most distant galaxies and the smallest stars ever seen. Before these discoveries were made, new large telescopes had to be built.

The most distant galaxies are called quasars. They were discovered in 1963 when astronomers noticed strong radio signals coming from small points in the sky. When the radio astronomer Maarten Schmidt from Mount Palomar Observatory looked at these points, he saw faint galaxies that could be seen only because they were shining brightly. These galaxies, or quasars, were the most powerful objects ever discovered, and are the most distant objects even seen. Some are over 13,000 million light-years away. They get their power from a huge black hole at their center.

A black hole is a region of space where the pull of gravity is so strong that even light cannot escape. When gas and dust fall into the black hole at the center of a quasar, they produce large amounts of light and heat. Although black holes are very small, they are extremely heavy. A black hole less than a centimeter across can weigh the same amount as the Earth. The black holes in the center of quasars may weigh up to 100 million times as much as our sun.

EXERCISE 1

> Adverb clauses are tested on the TOEFL® Test. The blanks in the sentences introduce adverb clauses. Complete the blanks with one of the following words:

before   when   because   although

1. New, large telescopes had to be built _____ important discoveries were made.

2. Quasars were discovered _____ astronomers noticed radio signals.

3. Maarten Schmidt saw faint galaxies _____ he looked at points in the sky.

4. The points could be seen _____ they shone brightly.

5. Light and heat are produced in the center of a quasar _____ gas and dust fall into it.

6. _____ black holes are small, they are extremely heavy.

EXERCISE 2

Choose the correct adverb clause marker from the parentheses.

1. Quasars are an important discovery (because/although) they are the most powerful objects ever seen.

2. The outer planets are cooler than the inner ones (as/whereas) they are further from the sun.

3. A black hole is a region of space (where/whenever) the gravitational pull is so strong that nothing can escape.

4. Radio waves from distant regions of space could be studied (while/after) the radio telescope was invented.

5. Telescopes see distant objects more clearly (whereas/because) radio telescopes collect radio waves.

6. Astronomers did not know about quasars (before/so that) radio telescopes were invented.

Grammar: Adverb Clauses

An adverb clause is a subordinate clause (dependent clause) with a subject and a verb. An adverb clause may come before or after the main clause (independent clause). When it comes before the main clause or at the beginning, it is usually separated from the main clause by a comma.

> ***When** Schmidt looked at the small points, he saw galaxies.*
> *Schmidt saw galaxies **when** he looked at the small points.*

ADVERB CLAUSE MARKERS

The following are some common words used to introduce an adverb clause.

1. Clause markers showing time:

after	by the time	until
as	once	when
before	since	whenever
as soon as	till	while

   *Meteors glow **as** they burn up in the atmosphere.*
   *It was difficult to observe the stars **before** the telescope was invented.*

2. Clause markers showing manner:

as	as if	as though	just as	like

   *Ancient peoples used the stars **as if** they were calendars.*
   *The Milky Way looks **as though** it is a faint band of light.*

3. Clause markers showing cause and effect:

because	since	as
now that	as long as	so that

   *Spacesuits were designed for astronauts **so that** they could breathe in space.*
   ***Since** some planets are too far away to send people, computer-operated space probes are sent.*

4. Clause markers showing opposition:

although	while
though	whereas
even though	

   *Most stars are white **while** some are colored.*
   ***Although** helium is rare on Earth, it is common in the universe.*

5. Clause markers showing condition:

if	in the event that	provided that	unless
even if	in case that		
only if			

   *You will see hundreds of stars **if** you look at the sky.*
   *You can study distant stars **provided that** you have a radio telescope.*

6. Clause markers showing purpose:

   so that   in order that   so (that)
                   in order to   (*That* is often omitted in spoken English.)

   *Astronomers improved telescopes **so that** they would discover more about the stars.*
   *Astronomers developed bigger and bigger telescopes **in order to** see the stars more clearly.*

7. Clause markers showing result:

   so . . . that   such . . . that

   *The stars are **so** far away **that** they cannot be seen without a telescope.*
   *The meteor hit the Earth with **such** force **that** it made a crater.*

8. Clause markers showing place:

   where   wherever   everywhere

   *There were stars **wherever** she looked.*
   *A crater was formed **where** the meteor hit the earth.*

Strategy

Look for the adverb clause markers and make sure that the adverb clause has both a *subject* and a *verb*.

Exercise 3

Underline the adverb clauses in the following sentences.

1. Although millions of meteors hit the earth's atmosphere, few of them are noticed.
2. A meteor leaves a bright trail as it streaks across the night sky.
3. Many meteorite falls are not noticed because they hit the earth in remote uninhabited areas.
4. The rate of the sun's radiation is so great that about 3 million tons of matter is converted into energy every second.
5. In ancient times, farmers planted crops when they saw a planet in the right part of the sky.
6. Even though a planet moves among the stars, it returns to the same part of the sky at the same time each year.

REDUCED ADVERB CLAUSES

Adverb clauses may be reduced to modifying phrases in the same way as adjective clauses are reduced to modifying phrases. A reduced adverb clause or modifying phrase does not contain a subject or a verb. It consists of a participle (present or past participle) or an adjective and clause marker (*although, when,* or *while*).

> *Full:* **After** *the space probes landed on Mars, they sent back pictures.*
> *Reduced:* **After landing on Mars, the space probes sent back pictures.**

> *Full:* **Although** *the moon rocks were expensive to obtain, they provided valuable information.*
> *Reduced:* **Although** *expensive to obtain, the moon rocks provided valuable information.*

An adverb clause may be changed to a modifying phrase only when the subject of the main clause and the adverb clause are the same.

> *Adverb clause:* **After** *the space probe landed on Venus, it mapped the surface.*
> *Modifying phrase:* **After** *landing on Venus, it mapped the surface.*

> *Adverb clause:* **After** *the space probe sent pictures, astronomers examined them.*
> *Modifying phrase: not possible*

PREPOSITIONAL EXPRESSIONS

Some prepositions have almost the same meaning as some of the clause markers, but they can be used only with nouns, noun phrases, or pronouns. They cannot be used with clauses.

> **Strategy**
>
> The following prepositions cannot be used in clauses: *because of, on account of, in case of, in spite of, despite, during*. When you see them, look for nouns, noun phrases, or pronouns in the distractors.

> *Cause/effect: Many of the planets are cratered* **because of** *meteor bombardment.*
>
> *Concession:* **In spite of** *the damage to the spacecraft, the astronauts got back to Earth safely.*
>
> *Condition:* **In case of** *contamination, special suits were worn.*
>
> *Time: Radio receivers were used* **during** *the Second World War.*

Exercise 4

The following sentences contain adverb clauses, reduced adverb clauses, and prepositional expressions. Circle the letter of the best answer that completes the sentence.

1. _____ the Ancient Chinese and Egyptians took astronomy seriously, the Greeks were the first to study the stars scientifically.
   - (A) Although
   - (B) Despite
   - (C) For
   - (D) Nevertheless

2. _____ the development of radio telescopes, distant regions of the Universe can be observed.
   - (A) The reason
   - (B) Because of
   - (C) Because
   - (D) It is because

3. Supernovas are caused _____ a star dies.
   - (A) as when
   - (B) that
   - (C) when
   - (D) it is

4. In 1987 a Canadian astronomer, Ian Shelton, spotted a supernova _____ looking at some photographs of the stars.
   - (A) was
   - (B) during
   - (C) as if
   - (D) while he was

5. _____ the 1987 supernova was so near, astronomers were able to study it carefully.
   - (A) Although
   - (B) Since
   - (C) It was
   - (D) As it was

6. _____ used simple instruments, the ancient Greek astronomer, Hipparchus, made the first accurate map of the stars 2100 years ago.
   - (A) Even though
   - (B) Even though he
   - (C) Nevertheless
   - (D) In spite of

On the TOEFL® Test

Adverb clauses are tested in the Structure part of the exam. In these items, any part of the adverb clause may be missing from the stem: it may be the clause marker, the subject, the verb, or other parts of the clause.

It is important to remember the following:

1. An adverb clause contains a subject and a verb.
2. A reduced adverb clause does not contain a subject and a verb.
3. Use the correct clause marker for the adverb clause.

   Example: _____ the solar system may seem big, it is a very small part of the universe.

   (A) Despite
   (B) Although
   (C) Even though it
   (D) Because

   The best answer is (B). (A) is incorrect because despite cannot be used in an adverb clause that has a subject and a verb. (C) is incorrect because it contains a subject, *it,* which is repeated again in the same clause. (D) is incorrect because it contains the wrong clause marker, giving reason instead of concession.

   Example: Ancient astronomers looked at the stars _____ could make predictions about the future.

   (A) they
   (B) so
   (C) so that they
   (D) as they

   The best answer is (C).

EXERCISES ON ADVERB CLAUSES

From the four words or phrases (A), (B), (C), or (D), choose the *one* that best completes the sentence.

1. Plexiglas is used in aircraft windows _____ is almost unbreakable.
   - (A) it
   - (B) because it
   - (C) because
   - (D) it because

2. American Indians grew popcorn for a few thousand years _____ arrival of European explorers in the 1400s.
   - (A) before
   - (B) before the
   - (C) since
   - (D) since they

3. The body uses proteins for energy _____ and fats cannot meet its energy needs.
   - (A) that carbohydrates
   - (B) when carbohydrates
   - (C) when they are carbohydrates
   - (D) that when carbohydrates

4. Spider monkeys are the best climbers in the jungle, _____ they do not have thumbs.
   - (A) nevertheless
   - (B) for
   - (C) despite
   - (D) although

5. Stars are hot bodies that give out light of their own, _____ planets shine only by reflecting light.
   - (A) however there are
   - (B) since
   - (C) whereas
   - (D) while they

6. A silkworm has glands that secrete a liquid that hardens into silk _____ comes into contact with air.
   - (A) as it
   - (B) when
   - (C) that
   - (D) it

7. _____ their immense distances, quasars have relatively high magnitudes.
   - (A) Whereas
   - (B) In spite of
   - (C) Although
   - (D) Yet

8. _____ body's activities put strains on certain bones, these bones strengthen themselves where the stress is greatest.
   - (A) That if
   - (B) That
   - (C) Because of
   - (D) If the

9. _____ Herman Melville is now regarded as one of America's finest writers, his greatest works mystified readers in his own lifetime.

(A) It is despite
(B) Despite
(C) Even though
(D) In spite of

10. _____ laser beam can be moved easily in all directions, it can be used for highly accurate cutting in industry.

(A) Because of
(B) It is a
(C) A
(D) As a

11. Limestone powder is added to animal feed _____ animals form good strong bones.

(A) why
(B) so that
(C) as a result of
(D) it is that

12. _____ sodium chloride (salt) is not used by sea-living organisms, it forms the dominant mineral in seawater.

(A) Since
(B) It is since
(C) Although
(D) Although it

CHAPTER 10: PREPOSITIONAL PHRASES

Introduction: Land Art

The land art movement first appeared in the U.S. in the late 1960s. Most of the work was created in a landscape setting, using whatever materials the artist came across. Part of its appeal is that in many cases the artist's work is quickly changed by the forces of nature. For example, Robert Smithson built a vast spiral jetty from earth and stones in the Great Salt Lake in Utah. Now deposits of salt and sulphur have completely changed the way it looks.

Some land artists welcomed such impermanence, because it meant their work could not be owned. As land art is often in wild, out-of-the-way places, it is rarely seen by the public. Many artists therefore record there activities in words, photographs, and so on.

Richard Long is one of the most famous and successful land artists. Much of his work consists of going for long, carefully planned walks in wild and lonely parts of the world. Sometimes he leaves his mark by making small changes to the landscape, such as forming a line of stones. More recently he has brought back objects from his walks and used them to make up sculptures in art galleries.

EXERCISE 1

Prepositional phrases are tested on the TOEFL® Test. Fill in the blanks with the correct preposition in the prepositional phrase.

1. It was _____ the 1960s _____ the United States that an art movement called land art started.

2. Land art is created _____ landscape setting _____ wild parts _____ the world.

3. Many times the artist's work is changed _____ nature.

4. Robert Smithson built a jetty _____ earth and stone _____ the Great Salt Lake _____ Utah.

5. Land art is found _____ out-of-reach places and is therefore not seen _____ many people.
6. Land artists often record their work _____ text or photographs.

Exercise 2

Correct the prepositions in the following sentences.

1. Richard Long leaves his mark by making changes with the landscape.
2. Richard Long brings back found objects of his walks.
3. Richard Long uses the objects in sculptures that are shown on art galleries.
4. Land art involves the artist going into nature, usually from a remote area.
5. The only record that remains of land art is photographic, sometimes combined of maps.

Grammar: Prepositional Phrases

The following are some common prepositions:

about	behind	in	through
above	below	in spite of	throughout
across	beneath	into	till
after	beside	like/unlike	to
against	between	near	toward
along	beyond	of	under
among	by	off	until
around	despite	on	up
as	down	out	upon
at	during	out of	with
because of	for	over	within
before	from	since	without

A prepositional phrase consists of a preposition and an object. The object may be a noun or a pronoun.

The work	is changed	by	nature	.
subject	verb	preposition	object of preposition	

The work	is changed	by	it	.
subject	verb	preposition	object of preposition	

The noun may have modifiers. In this case it is called a noun phrase.

Land art	is	in	wild	places	.
subject	verb	preposition	modifier	object of preposition	

Exercise 3

> **Mark the subject S, verb V, object O, and prepositional phrases PP in the following sentences.**

1. Artists have painted nature for centuries.
2. Richard Long recorded his work in different ways.
3. Most murals are painted in a naturalistic style.
4. The role of art in Western culture has changed in the last hundred years.
5. Futurism emerged in northern Italy before the First World War.
6. Some contemporary artists have rejected art galleries for political reasons.

> **Strategy**
>
> Look for the preposition and its object. Some words used as prepositions may not be used in a prepositional phrase.

Do not confuse a clause with a prepositional phrase.

> *Not a prepositional phrase:* **Because** *it changed, the work was impermanent.*
>
> *Prepositional phrase:* **Because of** *change, the work was impermanent.*

In other cases, a phrasal verb may cause confusion. A phrasal verb is a verb with one or two prepositions that together have a special meaning.

> *Not a prepositional phrase: The artist **ran across** an object.*
> *(the phrasal verb "run across" means to meet by accident)*
>
> *Prepositional phrase: The artist ran **across** the room to get a canvas.*

CHAPTER 10   PREPOSITIONAL PHRASES   97

Exercise 4

Underline the prepositional phrases in the following sentences.

1. The invention of photography in the 1820s encouraged artists to attempt even greater realism in their paintings.
2. As the nineteenth century wore on, some artists began to question the need for art to refer to the outside world.
3. By the nineteenth century, art dealers had begun to sell uncommissioned art to a wider public.
4. Monet was more concerned with expressing an almost mystical sense of communion with nature than with working spontaneously.
5. With the Industrial Revolution the landscape began to change more and more, and artists began to look into its negative and positive aspects.
6. Land art involves the artist going out into nature, usually in a remote area, and making his or her mark on it.

Strategy

Make sure you choose the correct preposition. To review prepositions, see Chapter 5.

Exercise 5

Choose the correct preposition to complete the sentence. Circle the letter of the best answer.

1. Artists have painted nature _____ centuries.
   (A) for
   (B) in
   (C) since
   (D) by

2. As Europe became more industrialized, art began to reflect a growing nostalgia _____ the old rural way of life.
   (A) in
   (B) for
   (C) of
   (D) to

3. By the twentieth century, artists were becoming less conventional _____ the way they portrayed landscape and nature in general.
   - (A) by
   - (B) as
   - (C) in
   - (D) for

4. Cubism was the result _____ a gradual process of change.
   - (A) on
   - (B) with
   - (C) in
   - (D) of

5. _____ with landscape, seventeenth century Dutch artists were the first to paint still lifes for their own sake.
   - (A) As
   - (B) In
   - (C) Since
   - (D) Beyond

6. The key role of the still life in modern art has been as a focus _____ technical and stylistic experiments.
   - (A) in
   - (B) on
   - (C) with
   - (D) to

7. Futurists were inspired _____ the dynamism of the machine age.
   - (A) with
   - (B) of
   - (C) by
   - (D) on

8. Op art became a very trendy movement and had a big influence _____ fashion.
   - (A) in
   - (B) to
   - (C) with
   - (D) on

On the TOEFL® Test

Prepositional phrases often appear at the beginning of a sentence but may also appear in other parts of the sentence.

The wrong preposition will appear in the distractors, or a clause may be used in the distractors without a connector to join it to the other clause.

It is important to remember that the subject of a sentence cannot be the object of a preposition.

Example: _____ turn of the century, the first art galleries and museums were built.
- (A) The
- (B) Around the
- (C) It was around the
- (D) When the

Choice (B) best completes the sentence. (A) is not correct as there is no connector joining the noun phrase "the turn of the century" with the rest of the sentence. (C) is a clause, but there is no connector joining it to the other clause. (D) looks like a subordinate clause but does not have a verb.

Example: _____ realistic painting or sculpture, emotion is expressed mainly through people's poses and expression.

(A) In a
(B) It is in a
(C) As
(D) A

The best answer is (A). (B) is a clause but there is no connector joining it to the other clause. (C) looks like a clause but does not have a verb. (D) is not correct as there is no connector joining it to the rest of the sentence.

EXERCISES ON PREPOSITIONAL PHRASES

From the four words or phrases, choose the *one* that best completes the sentence.

1. Camels store water _____ of fat in their humps.
    (A) with the form
    (B) in the form
    (C) by the form
    (D) form

2. Tears contain an antiseptic that helps protect our eyes _____ infection.
    (A) from bacterial
    (B) in bacterial
    (C) bacterial
    (D) with bacterial

3. So far only two other of our neighboring planets _____ the solar system have been visited by unmanned spacecraft.
    (A) by
    (B) that they are in
    (C) in
    (D) they are by

4. Many tropical orchids grow _____ branches of trees and have aerial roots that absorb water from the moist air around them.

   (A) of the
   (B) the
   (C) they are in the
   (D) in the

5. _____ compact disc, sound is stored as digital information in tiny pits on the surface.

   (A) On a
   (B) A
   (C) It is on a
   (D) Of a

6. Giraffes sleep only _____ an hour at a time and often do not sleep at all during twenty-four hours.

   (A) by
   (B) for
   (C) in
   (D) during

7. _____ were invented, patients had to be held down by force during painful operations.

   (A) As anesthetics
   (B) Because anesthetics
   (C) Before anesthetics
   (D) Anesthetics

8. The surface of a cactus is coated _____ waxy layer that prevents water from evaporating from the plant.

   (A) it is a
   (B) a
   (C) by a
   (D) with a

9. _____ eighteenth century, people began to realize that certain chemicals are affected and changed by light.

   (A) By the
   (B) The
   (C) It was the
   (D) That in the

10. In addition to their homes, the Pomo Indians of California built dance houses _____ religious ceremonies.

   (A) of
   (B) for
   (C) in which
   (D) were for

11. The wood of many pine species makes excellent pulp _____ manufacture of paper.

   (A) in
   (B) to
   (C) for the
   (D) the

12. The photos of the American Civil War made by Matthew Brady and his assistants rank _____ finest war pictures of all time.

   (A) the
   (B) in the
   (C) between the
   (D) among the

CHAPTER 11: COMPARATIVES AND SUPERLATIVES

Introduction: Violins

Violino Piccolo • Violin • Viola • Cello • Double Bass

For 100 or more years the violin was looked down on as a lesser musical instrument; music was not composed especially for it except in overtures to court pageants or background music for aristocratic drawing rooms. However, beginning around 1680 into the nineteenth century a succession of Italian violinist composers created an enormous amount of music for the violin—people such as Corelli, Vivaldi, Pugnani, Paganini, and Viotti.

The violin is the principal member of the violin family. The other members are the viola, the cello, and the double bass. The full-size violin, which is the smallest and highest pitched of the stringed instruments played with a bow, has a body size of fourteen inches. The viola is slightly larger than the violin, and it has a slightly richer but less brilliant tone. It is really an alto violin, and it fills the gap between the violin and the cello.

CHAPTER 11   COMPARATIVES AND SUPERLATIVES   103

The greatest of the violin makers was Antonio Stradivari, who was born in 1644. During his lifetime, Stradivari made over a thousand stringed instruments, of which about six hundred are still in existence.

Exercise 1

> Comparatives and superlatives are tested on the TOEFL® Test. Complete the sentences with the comparative or superlative form from the reading.

1. People looked down on the violin as a _____ musical instrument.
2. The violin is the _____ and _____ pitched of the stringed instruments played with a bow.
3. The viola is _____ than the violin.
4. The viola has a _____ tone than the violin.
5. But the viola has a less _____ tone than the violin.
6. Antonio Stradivari was the _____ violin maker.

Exercise 2

Fill in the blanks with one of the words in the box.

small   big   smaller   bigger   biggest   smallest

1. The double bass is the _____ of the violin family.
2. The cello is _____ than the double bass.
3. The cello is _____ than the viola.
4. The viola is not as _____ as the cello.
5. The violin is not as _____ as the viola.
6. The violin is the _____ of the violin family.

Grammar: Comparatives and Superlatives

THE COMPARATIVE AND SUPERLATIVE OF ADJECTIVES

There are three forms of comparison: the absolute (the base form of the adjective), the comparative, and the superlative.

1. The absolute form is used to describe a thing or person.

   *The violin is a **small** instrument.*

2. The comparative is used when comparing two things, or when comparing something(s) with other things.

   *The violin is **smaller than** the cello.*

3. The superlative is used when comparing more than two things, or when one in a group has the greatest amount of a quality.

   *The violin is **the smallest** of the violin family.*

Strategy

Check to see that the correct form of the comparative and superlative is used where needed on the TOEFL® Test.

---

a. The comparative and the superlative of one-syllable adjectives are formed by adding *-er* and *-est* to the absolute.

Absolute	Comparative	Superlative
small	smaller	smallest
high	higher	highest

b. The comparative and the superlative of adjectives of three or more syllables are formed by adding *more* and *most*.

Absolute	Comparative	Superlative
brilliant	more brilliant	most brilliant
important	more important	most important

CHAPTER 11 COMPARATIVES AND SUPERLATIVES

> **Strategy**
>
> Check to see that the absolute, comparative, and superlative structures are formed correctly in TOEFL® Test questions.

c. Some adjectives ending in *-er, -y,* or *-le* form comparatives and superlatives by adding *-er* or *-est* to the absolute form ("y" changes to "i").

Absolute	Comparative	Superlative
early	earlier	earliest
simple	simpler	simplest

THE COMPARATIVE AND SUPERLATIVE OF ADVERBS

The forms used for the comparison of adjectives are also used for the comparison of adverbs.

d. For the comparative and superlative forms of all one-syllable adverbs use *-er* and *-est*.

Absolute	Comparative	Superlative
fast	faster	fastest
early	earlier	earliest

e. For all other adverbs use *more* and *most*.

Absolute	Comparative	Superlative
slowly	more slowly	most slowly
commonly	more commonly	most commonly

f. The following are irregular comparatives and superlatives of adjectives and adverbs.

Absolute	Comparative	Superlative
good (adj)	better	best
well (adv)	better	best
bad (adj)	worse	worst
badly (adv)	worse	worst
little (adj/adv)	less	least
many (adj)	more	most
much (adj/adv)	more	most
far (adj/adv)	farther	farthest
	further	furthest
late (adv)	later	last
old (adj)	older	oldest
	elder	eldest

g. The comparative form *less* and the superlative from *least* are used with both adjectives and adverbs to show that something does not have as much as something else.

*This mass-produced violin is **less** expensive.*

*Of the mass-produced violins, this one is the **least** expensive.*

OTHER FORMS OF THE COMPARATIVE

1. *As . . . as / Not as . . . as / Not so . . . as*

   When things that are equal are compared, the following forms can be used:

   as . . . as
   not as (positive) as
   not so (positive) as

   *There are not **as** many violin makers today **as** there were in the past.*

   *Playing the violin is **not as** difficult **as** you might think.*

2. *The Double Comparative*

   The double comparative is used to show parallel increase or decrease.

   the + comparative . . . *the* + comparative

   ***The more** he plays, **the more** he improves.*
   ***The shorter** the string, **the higher** the note.*

3. *As and Like*

   In a simple comparison, *like* is used before a noun or pronoun.

   *You play the cello with a bow **like** the violin.*

   If a verb follows the noun and pronoun, *as* must be used.

   *You play the cello with a bow **as** you do the violin.*

CHAPTER 11 COMPARATIVES AND SUPERLATIVES

Exercise 3

> **Underline the comparatives that are incorrect in the following sentences.**

1. Stretching a string more tightly gives a highest note.
2. The violin is probably the most importantest of all orchestral instruments.
3. The viols are bowed strings that are more older than the violin family.
4. The viols do not have as bright a sound the violin family.
5. The heavier the string, the low the note it sounds.
6. Small violins have short strings than full-sized instruments, but they play the same notes.
7. Andres Segovia is the more famous classical guitarist in the world.
8. It is said that a special varnish used on a violin helps to produce the more beautiful tone.

On the TOEFL® Test

In the Structure section, adjectives are usually compared. The forms *as . . . as, the more . . . the more, similar to, different from, unlike,* and so on may appear in this section.

Example: _____ tilted toward the sun, the more heat it receives and the hotter it is.

(A) As more as the earth is
(B) The more the earth is
(C) The earth is more than
(D) The earth is most

The best choice is (B); it should have the construction *the more . . . the more.*

In the Written Expression section, the three forms of the comparative and superlative (the absolute, comparative, or superlative) may be used incorrectly.

Example: The Great Plains region of the United States suffered one of
                                                                   A
the worse droughts in history from 1931 to 1938.
    B   C   D

The best answer is (B); the sentence does not compare two groups and therefore, the superlative *worst* is required.

Exercises on Comparatives and Superlatives

From the four words or phrases (A), (B), (C), or (D), choose the *one* that best completes the sentence.

1. Temperature, the simplest weather element to measure, is probably _____ used than any other kind of data.
   (A) more frequently
   (B) most frequently
   (C) as frequently
   (D) frequently

2. Paprika is _____ red or cayenne pepper, and it has a sweeter taste.
   (A) least biting
   (B) less biting than
   (C) lesser biting than
   (D) less as

3. The foods that contain _____ are made of animal fat whereas vegetables have the least energy.
   (A) as much energy as
   (B) the more energy
   (C) the most energy
   (D) more energy than

4. Albert Einstein's contributions to scientific theory were _____ those of Galileo and Newton.
   (A) important than
   (B) more important
   (C) the most important
   (D) as important as

5. Impalas cannot move as _____ cheetahs, but they are more efficient runners.
   (A) faster than
   (B) fast as
   (C) fast
   (D) are fast as

6. Apart from Pluto, the outer planets _____ the inner planets and are made mainly of lighter materials such as hydrogen and helium.
   (A) are larger than
   (B) are the largest
   (C) larger than
   (D) are large

CHAPTER 11 COMPARATIVES AND SUPERLATIVES   109

> **From the four underlined words or phrases, (A), (B), (C), or (D), identify the *one* that is not correct.**

7. During the 1700s, Philadelphia developed into the most wealthy city in
      A   B   C
   the American colonies.
           D

8. According to Freud, the mind experiences more unconsciouser than
        A   B   C
   conscious activity.
      D

9. Eleanor Roosevelt was one of the most activest and influential first
                        A   B   C   D
   ladies.

10. The Sahara Desert in Africa is by far the most large desert in the world,
                                 A   B
    covering an area nearly as big as the United States.
                C   D

11. Peanuts are closely related to peas than to nuts.
       A   B   C   D

12. Most evergreens have needle-like leaves that require least water than
       A   B   C
    regular leaves.
       D

CHAPTER 12 CONJUNCTIONS

Introduction: The Soya Bean's Industrial Uses

Soya is not only used in the manufacture of food for human and animal consumption but also in a variety of industrial processes. These range from the manufacture of adhesives and plastics to dynamite and waterproofing preparations.

For many years soya bean oil has been used in the manufacture of paints, both for domestic and industrial use. It is also used in the printing industry in printing inks, adhesives, and paper. In the United States the soya bean is used in the brewing industry to help the yeast ferment and enhance the flavor of beer.

Soya is even used in fire-fighting as a foam agent. When mixed with water and air it produces the fire-fighting foam. Water might put out the surface flames, but the fire could still be burning underneath. Fire-fighting foam on the other hand clings to most surfaces and does not drain as quickly as water. If oil has caught fire, the foam floats on the surface and smothers the flames.

Glycerine, which is a byproduct of vegetable oils including soya, is used in nearly every industry. It is an ingredient in many medicines including cough mixtures and is also a basic medium in toothpaste. Glycerine is not only used in glues to prevent quick drying, but also in the manufacture of explosives. No doubt as research and experiments continue, even more uses for this versatile crop will be found.

EXERCISE 1

Conjunctions are tested on the TOEFL® Test. Fill in the blanks with one of the following conjunctions: *and, but,* or *or.*

1. Soya is used in the printing industry in printing inks, adhesives, _____ paper.

2. In the brewing industry soya helps the yeast to ferment _____ enhances the flavor of the beer.

3. When soya is mixed with water _____ air it produces a fire-fighting foam.

4. Water might put out the flames _____ the fire would still be burning underneath.

5. Fire-fighting foam clings to surfaces _____ does not drain as quickly as water.

6. Glycerine is used in many medicines including cough mixtures _____ is the basic medium in toothpaste.

Exercise 2

> Correct the mistakes with the following constructions in the sentences: *not only . . . but also* or *both . . . and.*

1. Soya is used not only in many food processes and also in many industrial processes.

2. Soya has been used in the manufacture of paints for both industrial or domestic use.

3. Glycerine is used not only in glues but in the manufacture of explosives.

4. Soya is used in the manufacture of food for both human consumption but also animal consumption.

5. American farmers have been encouraged to grow more soya not only because the export market has expanded also because the demand at home has increased.

6. The ancient Chinese used the soya bean for both food and also medicine.

Grammar: Conjunctions

Conjunctions are tested in both the Structure and Written Expression sections. The two kinds of conjunctions tested are:

a. Coordinating conjunctions

b. Correlative conjunctions

COORDINATING CONJUNCTIONS

Coordinating conjunctions connect words or phrases that have the same function in a sentence. The coordinating conjunctions tested on the TOEFL® Test are *and, but, or,* and *so*.

1. ***And***

    And joins two or more words, phrases, or clauses of similar function and is used to show addition.

    *Like peas **and** broad beans, soya beans grow in pods.*

    *The plant is ready for harvesting when the leaves turn yellow and drop off, **and** the pods and stems dry out.*

    Note: When *and* joins two subjects, the verb is plural.

    *Soya beans and peas **have** pods.*

2. ***But***

    But joins two or more words, phrases, or clauses and is used to show contrast.

    *In the U.S. soya is not harvested by hand **but** my machine.*

    *Soya is not a new discovery **but** is one of the oldest crops grown in the Orient.*

3. ***Or***

    Or joins two or more words, phrases, or clauses. It is used to give a choice.

    *The beans may be yellow, green, brown, **or** mottled.*

    *After being chilled, the margarine is packed into tubs **or** cut in blocks.*

4. ***So***

    So joins a clause. It does not join single words or phrases. *So* is used to show effect.

    *The soya bean is versatile, **so** it is grown widely.*

CHAPTER 12 CONJUNCTIONS

> **Strategy**
>
> Although other conjunctions are not tested directly in the Structure section, some conjunctive adverbs like *moreover, nevertheless,* and *therefore* may appear in the distractors, in which case they will be the wrong choice. However, when these words appear with conjunctions like *and, but,* or *or,* they may be used to join clauses.
>
> **Example:** and therefore
> but nevertheless
> and moreover

CORRELATIVE CONJUNCTIONS

Like coordinating conjunctions, these words are used to join words, phrases, and clauses. Correlative conjunctions or paired conjunctions appear in two parts:

either . . . or
neither . . . nor
both . . . and
not only . . . but also
whether . . . or

Each of the pair of words should be followed by a word of the same grammatical form.

Either (noun) ***or*** (noun)
Not only (adj) ***but also*** (adj)

1. ***Either . . . or***

   Either . . . or is used to indicate alternatives.

   *Soya can be used in **either** fish feed **or** chicken feed.*

   The subject closest to the verb will determine if the verb is singular or plural.

2. ***Neither . . . nor***

   Neither . . . nor is used to indicate negative alternatives.

   *Soya is dangerous to **neither** humans **nor** animals.*

   The subject closest to the verb will determine if the verb is singular or plural.

3. **Both . . . and**

   Both . . . and indicates addition.

   *Soya protein isolate is used in **both** meat **and** fish products.*

   Subjects connected with *both . . . and* take a plural verb.

4. **Not only . . . but also**

   Not only . . . but also emphasizes addition.

   *Soya is **not only** the most efficient **but also** the least costly source of protein.*

   The *not only* clause must come before the phrase it refers to. The subject closest to the verb will determine if the verb is singular or plural.

5. **Whether . . . or**

   Whether . . . or indicates a condition.

   ***Whether** it is in the print of a newspaper **or** the food we eat, our lives are touched by soya.*

EXERCISE 3

Circle the letter of the word or phrase that correctly completes the sentence.

1. Around 1910 chemists and manufacturers came to recognize the value of the soya bean, _____ the great soya processing industry was born.

   (A) with
   (B) and
   (C) but
   (D) or

2. The expansion of the industry was not only due to the world shortage of edible oils, _____ to the Second World War, which put traditional sources of protein in short supply.

   (A) but also
   (B) as well as
   (C) and so
   (D) but also as

3. Research began in the United States into ways of using soya meal for human food, _____ it was not until the 1950s that the first edible soya protein was produced.

   (A) nevertheless
   (B) or
   (C) but
   (D) and

4. The soya plant is an annual, _____ new seeds must be planted every year.

   (A) such
   (B) and since
   (C) while
   (D) so

5. The soya plant is attacked by both fungus disease _____ virus disease.

   (A) and
   (B) and also
   (C) but also
   (D) or

6. The ground bran from soya is used either in breakfast cereals _____ in animal feed.

   (A) nor
   (B) or
   (C) and also
   (D) and

7. Soya protein isolate is used where a high level of protein is required, whether it is dietetic _____ hospital food.

   (A) or
   (B) nor
   (C) and also
   (D) but also

8. Today most margarine is made of vegetable oils _____ originally it was made from animal fats.

   (A) except
   (B) but
   (C) nevertheless
   (D) thus

On the TOEFL® Test

In the Structure section errors with conjunctions include:

1. Coordinating conjunctions:

   and (addition)
   but (contrast)
   or (choice)

2. Correlative conjunctions:

   either . . . or
   neither . . . nor
   both . . . and
   not only . . . but also
   whether . . . or

Since correlative conjunctions are in two parts, there is usually an error in one of the parts.

Example: Soya is an important crop used in _____ food and industrial processes.

(A) either
(B) both
(C) and
(D) just

The best answer is (B); the correct construction is *both . . . and;* the other distractors do not follow this construction.

In the Written Expression section errors with conjunctions also include:

1. Coordinating conjunctions: and, but, or
2. Correlative conjunctions: either . . . or, neither . . . nor, both . . . and, not only . . . but also, whether . . . or

   Example: <u>Soya</u> beans <u>contain</u> not only vitamins <u>and</u> also <u>important</u>
           A   B   C   D
   minerals.

The correct answer is (C); the correct construction is *not only . . . but also.*

EXERCISES ON CONJUNCTIONS

From the four words or phrases (A), (B), (C), or (D), choose the *one* that best completes the sentence.

1. Both diamond _____ graphite are made of the same element, which is carbon.

   (A) and
   (B) except
   (C) together
   (D) both

2. Blinking helps keep the surface of the eye clean _____ moist.

   (A) to
   (B) or
   (C) and
   (D) so

3. Normally, piranhas swim alone and feed on smaller fish _____ on seeds in the water.

   (A) but
   (B) either
   (C) instead
   (D) or

4. Most rodents eat grain, seeds, and nuts, _____ some eat almost anything.

   (A) contrary
   (B) they
   (C) but
   (D) instead

5. Fungi do not absorb sunlight but use animals and plants, _____ dead and living, as their source of food.

   (A) furthermore
   (B) both
   (C) together
   (D) besides

6. Recently doctors warned that too much animal fat in the diet can lead to heart disease, _____ special types of margarine made with vegetable oils are becoming popular.

   (A) because
   (B) so
   (C) and since
   (D) except

> **From the four underlined words or phrases, identify the *one* that is not correct.**

7. <u>Peppermint</u> originated in Europe, <u>but</u> the early English colonists
     A   B
   <u>brought</u> <u>it</u> to North America.
     C   D

8. The <u>central</u> core of the earth is <u>made</u> of both very hot <u>or</u> dense <u>material</u>.
          A   B   C   D

9. <u>Many</u> meteorite falls go <u>unnoticed</u> <u>because</u> they either happen at night
    A   B   C
   <u>nor</u> they hit the earth in uninhabited areas.
    D

10. Octopuses have not only large brains <u>and</u> also <u>a</u> <u>well-developed</u> nervous
            A   B   C   D
    system.

11. Most scholars <u>are</u> unsure whether the wheel was <u>first</u> used <u>by</u> potters in
             A   B   C
    Mesopotamia <u>and</u> in the central or eastern parts of Europe.
                  D

12. Compact discs <u>are</u> <u>affected</u> neither <u>by</u> scratching <u>and</u> by dust.
                  A   B   C   D

CHAPTER 13
PARALLEL STRUCTURE

Introduction: Vitamin C

In the past people suffered from a disease called scurvy. Their gums bled, their skin became rough, their wounds did not heal, and their muscles wasted away. The cause of these symptoms was a lack of vitamin C; people ate preserved meats and foods and could not get fresh vegetables and fruits.

The best sources of vitamin C are oranges, lemons, grapefruit, cantaloupes, strawberries, and fresh vegetables. These fruits must be fresh because vitamin C is destroyed by heat, storage, or exposure to air.

Although today more people take vitamin C pills than any other supplement, some people still have scurvy, including some of the elderly, alcoholics, and the chronically ill.

Research shows that vitamin C reduces the severity of colds and can help prevent cancer. There is also evidence that vitamin C prevents heart disease, speeds wound healing, helps prevent gum disease, and helps protect us from pollutants such as cigarette smoke. Some recent research also shows that vitamin C has a positive effect on some mental disorders and increases life span.

Exercise 1

> **Parallel Structure is tested on the TOEFL® Test. Complete the following sentences with words from the passage that have parallel structure.**

1. In the past, people got scurvy because they did not get _____ and _____.

2. When people got scurvy their _____, _____, _____, and _____.

3. Vitamin C is destroyed by _____, _____, or _____.

4. Today some people like _____, _____, and _____ have scurvy.

118

CHAPTER 13   PARALLEL STRUCTURE   119

5. There is evidence that vitamin C prevents heart disease, _____, _____, and _____.

6. Recent research shows that vitamin C helps some mental disorders and _____.

Exercise 2

> **Correct the claims for and against vitamin C supplements by putting them in the same form. Use the simple present tense for the verbs.**

For

_____ 1. Lowering cholesterol and fights heart disease.

_____ 2. Helps to keep good eyesight.

_____ 3. Protects against smoking and various pollutants.

_____ 4. Diabetes fights.

_____ 5. Will fight gum disease.

_____ 6. Strengthen immunity against colds.

Against

_____ 1. Is a waste of money because the body excretes excess vitamin C.

_____ 2. Will cause kidney stones or gout in some people.

_____ 3. May cause diarrhea and stomach cramps in some people.

_____ 4. Cause stones in the bladder in some people.

Grammar: Parallel Structure

Many sentences present information in a series or list. The series may have two, three, or more parts that all have the same grammatical structure. This is known as parallel structure.

> **Strategy**
>
> Make sure that words in a sequence have the same form. These may be nouns, adjectives, verbs, adverbs, phrases, and so on.

a. Series Containing Nouns, Adjectives, Adverbs, or Phrases

Nouns: Vitamin C is destroyed by **heat, storage,** or **exposure** to air.

Adjectives: The criticism that taking vitamin C supplements is a waste of money is considered to be **inaccurate** and **unwarranted** by some.

Verbs: There is evidence that vitamin C **prevents** heart disease, **speeds** wound healing, and **helps** gum disease.

Adverbs: Vitamin supplements can be prepared **naturally** and **synthetically.**

Phrases: Large amounts of vitamin C can be bought **in the form of crystals,** or **in the form of granules.**

b. Gerunds or Infinitives

Infinitive: When people get scurvy their cells tend **to disintegrate** and **to fall apart.**

Gerund: Claims for vitamin C such as **reducing** stress and **improving** athletic performance have not been scientifically demonstrated.

c. Correlative Conjunctions

both . . . and   neither . . . nor
either . . . or   not only . . . but also

Both fruits ***and*** vegetables are rich sources of vitamin C.
Since vitamin A is not created in the body, it must be supplied by ***either*** food ***or*** supplements.

EXERCISE 3

The following sentences contain a series. Underline the parallel structure, then say what type of series the sentence contains by using the following abbreviations: *nouns* **(N),** *verbs* **(V),** *adjectives* **(ADJ),** *adverbs* **(ADV).**

1. Vitamin E protects against heart disease, prevents cancer, and fights skin problems.

2. The mineral fluoride is found naturally in soils, water, plants, and animal tissue.

3. The tomato plant needs a long growing season and light, rich, well-drained soil.

4. Vitamin E is being employed slowly but steadily in medicine in an expanding range of ailments.

5. Studies have shown that vitamin C can reduce the severity and length of colds, but not the number of colds a person gets.

6. If you do not have enough iron, you can suffer from anemia, which makes you pale, tired, and weak.

EXERCISE 4

Underline the errors in parallel structure in the following sentences.

1. Iron-deficiency anemia has been implicated in emotion, social, and learning difficulties in infants, adolescents, and adults.

2. All "B" vitamins are needed for a healthy appetite, energy production in cells, healthy nervous, and skin.

3. Some vitamins may cause toxic, allergy reactions in some people.

4. Symptoms of a mild case of vitamin C deficiency may be weakness, irritable, loss of weight, and apathy.

5. Claims that vitamin C will prevent, relief, or cure colds and winter illnesses are unwarranted, according to Hodges.

6. Magnesium deficiency is characterized by loss of appetite, nausea, confusing, loss of coordination, and tremors.

EXERCISE 5

Identify and correct errors in parallel structure related to *infinitives* and *gerunds* in the following sentences.

1. Some people take vitamin E to relieve muscular cramps, to extend life span, and fighting skin problems.

2. The Nobel laureate Dr. Linus Pauling persistently claimed that vitamin C is effective in preventing and alleviating colds and to treat cancer.

3. Many food processes such as drying, flavoring, canning, and to tenderize may add salt.

4. It is important to select foods that are in their best state, storing them properly, and prepare them to ensure the maximum retention of vitamin C.

5. Avoiding the purchase of foods with salt content while marketing or to eat out is helpful.

6. The major function of vitamin D is to ensure an adequate supply of calcium and phosphorus in the bones, to prevent rickets in children, and maintaining good levels of calcium and phosphorus in the blood.

EXERCISE 6

Identify and correct errors in parallel structure related to *correlative conjunctions* in the following sentences.

1. Very large intakes of any of the essential nutrients may result in both undesirable toxic symptoms and seriously side effects.

2. Minerals in the cell influence not only the vital processes of oxidation but also secreting and growth.

3. Many people feel that both frozen and can fruits and vegetables are inferior to fresh produce.

4. Canned food can be kept neither for unlimited lengths of time nor any temperature.

5. Fruit grown either sheltered from sunlight or growing in a season of many rainy days will not have much vitamin C.

6. Good peaches should be neither too hard, nor too softness.

On the TOEFL® Test

Parallel structure is tested in both the Structure section and the Written Expression section. Words in parallel structure must have the same form in a sequence. In the Structure section look for words from the choice of (A), (B), (C), and (D) that follow the same form as in the main sentence.

> **Example:** Vitamin C boosts immunity against colds, _____ asthma, and helps maintain good vision.

(A) counteracting
(B) counteracts
(C) will counteract
(D) it is counteractive to

The best answer is (B) because it is parallel with the other items in the sequence: *boosts* immunity and *helps* maintain good vision. Answer choices (A), (C), and (D) are not in the simple present tense and therefore are not parallel.

In the Written Expression section, sentences have the same errors in parallel structure as in the Structure section. Sentences have a sequence of three or more items, but here one of the items in the sequence is not grammatically parallel with the other items in the sequence.

Example: Symptoms of mild vitamin C deficiency may be <u>weakness</u>,
                                                          A
<u>irritability</u>, <u>losing weight</u>, and <u>apathy</u>.
      B   C   D

The best answer choice is (C) because it is not parallel with the other items in the series: losing is a gerund whereas the other items are nouns.

EXERCISES ON PARALLEL STRUCTURE

> **From the four underlined words or phrases (A), (B), (C), or (D), identify the *one* that is not correct.**

1. In the <u>human body</u>, phosphorus compounds are found chiefly in
           A
   the <u>bones</u>, <u>brain</u>, and <u>nervous</u>.
         B   C   D

2. Pipelines are continually inspected for leaks and <u>for damage</u> caused by
                                                       A
   such conditions as <u>freezing temperatures</u>, <u>heavy rain</u>, and <u>soil erode</u>.
                        B   C   D

3. <u>The sounds</u> produced by a <u>musical instrument</u>, <u>to whistle</u>, or a siren
     A   B   C
   have seven <u>frequencies</u> at the same time.
                D

4. Plastics used to make textiles can <u>be drawn</u> into <u>fine threads</u>, then
                                        A   B
   <u>woven</u> or <u>knit</u> into fabrics.
     C   D

5. Insufficient <u>protein</u> in the diet may cause a <u>lack of energy</u>,
                  A   B
   stunted <u>growth</u>, and <u>lowering resistance to disease</u>.
             C   D

6. Chemical substances called hormones, many of which are proteins,
         A
   control such processes as growth, develop, and reproduction.
                         B   C   D

From the four words or phrases (A), (B), (C), or (D), choose the *one* that best completes the sentence.

---

7. To qualify as a language, a communication system must have the features of meaningfulness, _____, and productivity.
   - (A) displacement
   - (B) to displace
   - (C) displacing
   - (D) to be displaced

8. Many mental disorders are believed to result from a combination of emotional, _____, and biological factors.
   - (A) society
   - (B) social
   - (C) socially
   - (D) to be social

9. A neuron cell can not only receive messages from sense organs, but it can also _____.
   - (A) to transmit messages throughout the body.
   - (B) by transmitting messages throughout the body
   - (C) transmit messages throughout the body
   - (D) a transmitter of messages throughout the body

10. Morse invented a code in which letters, numbers, and _____ are changed into short and long signals called dots and dashes.
    - (A) punctuate
    - (B) punctuating
    - (C) to punctuate
    - (D) punctuation

11. Hormones have many jobs, from promoting bodily growth to _____ to regulating metabolism.
    - (A) aid digestion
    - (B) aiding digestion
    - (C) be of aid to digestion
    - (D) an aid of digestion

12. Thomas Malthus claimed that disease, war, famine, and _____ act as checks on population growth.
    - (A) moral restraining
    - (B) morally restrain
    - (C) moral restraint
    - (D) by moral restraint

CHAPTER 14 WORD ORDER

Introduction: Computers

It is relatively easy for computers to speak. A computer that says "please" and "thank you" in the right places is no miracle of science, but recognizing the words that make up normal, continuous human speech is another matter.

Not until now have computers been programmed to react to a range of spoken commands. Until recently it was thought that computers would have to be programmed to the accent and speech habits of each user, and only then would be able to respond accurately to their master's or mistress's voice. Now rapid progress is being made with systems programmed to adapt easily to each new speaker.

The IBM Tangora system, under development at the end of the 1980s, was claimed to recognize a spoken vocabulary of 20,000 words with 95 percent accuracy. The system includes a processor that can make informed guesses as to what is a likely sentence. The system has been programmed not only with grammatical rules, but also with an analysis of a vast quantity of office correspondence. On the basis of this information, the machine can calculate the probability of one particular word following another.

Statistical probability is necessary for computers to interpret not only speech but also visual data. Security systems can distinguish between faces they have been taught to recognize, but never has a computer been able to match a human's ability to make sense of a three-dimensional scene by identifying all objects in it.

Exercise 1

> **Word order is tested on the TOEFL® Test. Correct the word order in the following sentences.**

1. For computers to speak relatively easy is.
2. Until recently it thought was computers would have to be programmed to the accent and speech habits of the user.
3. It is claimed that the IBM Tangora system can recognize a vocabulary spoken of 20,000 words.
4. Statistical probability necessary is for computers to interpret not only speech but visual data as well.
5. Up to now have computers not been programmed to react to a range of spoken commands.
6. The machine can calculate the probability of one word particular following another.

Exercise 2

> **With sentences starting with a negative word, word order is reversed. Complete the sentences with the correct negative word.**

1. (Not until/Never) now have computers been programmed to react to spoken commands.
2. (Never/Not only) has a computer been able to match a human's ability to make sense of a three-dimensional scene.
3. (Only/Not only) are grammatical rules programmed into the computer but also an analysis of office correspondence.
4. (Not until/Scarcely) recently was it thought that computers would have to be programmed to the speech and accent of the user.
5. (Only/No sooner than) recently has progress been made in recognizing human speech.
6. (Nor/Not only) can a computer recognize a three-dimensional scene by identifying all objects in it.

Grammar: Word Order
INVERSION

In English the usual word order is

> subject (S) + verb (V) + object (O)

In some situations the order is changed, and the verb is placed before the subject.

1. In a question the subject follows the aux-word or verb.

   Usual word order: You are using a computer.
                             S   V   O

   Inversion: Are you using a computer?
                      S   O

2. When there is a prepositional phrase indicating place at the beginning of a sentence, inversion occurs.

Usual word order:	*The workings of the computer are **inside** the system unit.*
Inversion:	***Inside** the system unit are the workings of the computer.*
Usual word order:	*The computer programs are fed **into** the computer.*
Inversion:	***Into** the comuter are fed the computer programs.*

3. When the conditional "if" has been omitted, inverted word order is correct.

Usual word order:	*If I had used a computer it would have been finished now.*
Inversion:	*Had I used a computer, it would have been finished now.*
Usual word order:	*If you should need the information, it will be in the computer.*
Inversion:	*Should you need the information, it will be in the computer.*

4. When a statement begins with a negative word or phrase, inversion occurs.

When the words below begin a sentence or an independent clause, there is a change in word order.

never	only
nor	only after
neither	only once
hardly ever	only once
no sooner than	only in this way
not often only	only then
not only . . . as well	rarely
not only . . . but also	scarcely
not until	seldom
nowhere	under no circumstances
on no account	so

Usual word order: I will **never** again write on a typewriter.
Inversion: **Never** again will I write on a typewriter.
Usual word order: The computer **not only** examines information **but also** performs logical operations.
Inversion: **Not only** does the computer examine information **but** it **also** performs logical operations.

Exercise 3

Rewrite the sentences with inverted word order.

1. If you should make an error, it can be corrected easily.
2. Information is stored on a magnetic disk.
3. If he had been more careful, we would not have lost all that data.
4. The computer not only stores information but also distributes it.
5. Personal computers no sooner were invented than typewriters began to be replaced.
6. The impact of the computer has been strongly felt only recently.

OTHER WORDS REVERSED ON THE TOEFL® TEST

> **Strategy**
> Be aware that other words such as nouns and adjectives, adverbs, and adjectives, and so on are reversed in order in the Written Expression section.

Other words that are reversed in order that appear in the Written Expression section may include:

1. Noun/adjective

    Correct: important information
    Error: information important

2. Adjective/adverb

    Correct: an extremely accurate document
    Error: an accurate extremely document

3. Relative pronoun/preposition

    Correct: It has transformed the way in which people work.
    Error: It has transformed the way which in people work.

4. Enough plus adjective

    Correct: simple enough
    Error: enough simple

5. Indirect questions

    Correct: He asked how expensive it was.
    Error: He asked how expensive was it.

6. Participle/adverb

    Correct: an accurately typed document
    Error: a typed accurately document

7. Adjective/adverb

    Correct: increasingly important machine
    Error: important increasingly machine

EXERCISE 4

Identify one of the four underlined words or phrases (A), (B), (C), or (D) that is not correct.

1. The development of <u>voice</u> recognition <u>will</u> enable the computer
                          A   B
   <u>to respond</u> to <u>commands spoken</u>.
      C   D

2. The direction <u>which in</u> computers <u>are</u> moving in education is what we
                     A   B
   <u>learn</u> rather than <u>how</u> we learn.
     C   D

3. The keyboard with <u>alphabet</u> keys is <u>enough easy</u> <u>to use</u> to give <u>program</u>
                        A   B   C   D
   instructions to the computer.

4. Computers <u>are</u> <u>machines flexible</u> that <u>can adapt</u> to a <u>wide</u> variety of
            A   B   C   D
   tasks.

5. Computers <u>can</u> <u>also</u> produce <u>complex</u> and <u>original highly</u> music.
            A B   C   D

6. Images and sounds <u>often</u> <u>added are</u> to games <u>to make</u> them
                   A   B   C
   <u>more realistic</u> and more exciting.
        D

On the TOEFL® Test

In the Written Expression section, word order problems involve two words in reverse order. These words may be:

1. Adjective/noun
2. Main verb/auxiliary
3. Enough/adjective
4. Indirect question word order
5. Adjective/adverb

6. Participle/adverb

7. Relative pronoun/preposition

   Example: A <u>pocket</u> computer is <u>generally</u> <u>enough</u> small to fit into a
                 A   B   C
   pocket or a <u>small</u> case.
             D

The best answer is (C); the correct word order is adjective + enough: *small enough.*

In the Structure section, word order problems involve sentences beginning with negative words or conditionals.

   Example: _____ used for making decisions in the business world, but also for forecasting and planning.

   (A) Not only are computers
   (B) Computers are
   (C) Not only computers are
   (D) Only computers are

The correct answer is (A); reversed subject/verb order is needed in sentences beginning with the negative *not only . . . but also* construction.

EXERCISES ON INVERSION

> **From the four underlined words or phrases, identify the *one* that is not correct.**

1. In the nineteenth century, Ada Lovelace <u>devised</u> several <u>computer</u>
                                           A   B
   programs for a calculating machine <u>which in</u> coded cards <u>were used</u>.
                                        C   D

2. In 1821, Babbage found <u>it</u> difficult <u>to make</u> a machine's parts
                             A   B
   <u>enough accurate</u> <u>to prevent</u> errors in calculation.
         C   D

3. <u>Does seldom a</u> <u>computer</u> <u>make</u> a <u>mistake</u>.
      A   B   C   D

4. Science <u>is</u> the process of <u>gathering</u> knowledge and answering <u>questions</u>
          A   B   C
   about the world and how works <u>it</u>.
                                  D

5. The telescope <u>first</u> used <u>was</u> in 1608 <u>as</u> a war weapon <u>to spy</u> on enemy
                          A   B   C   D
ships.

6. <u>When</u> the weather <u>is</u> warm, or during exercise <u>strenuous</u>, the sweat
     A   B   C
glands <u>increase</u> their production.
          D

From the four words or phrases (A), (B), (C), or (D), choose the *one* that best completes the sentence.

---

7. _____ reptiles hunt at temperatures of 12°C or below.
   (A) Seldom do
   (B) Do seldom
   (C) Do
   (D) Seldom

8. _____ learn during their sleep by listening to tape recordings.
   (A) People rarely can
   (B) Can people rarely
   (C) Rarely can people
   (D) Can rarely people

9. _____ continental crust older than 200 million years.
   (A) It is nowhere the
   (B) Nowhere is the
   (C) Is nowhere the
   (D) Is the nowhere

10. _____ lay its eggs in the sand on the beach that it goes back to the sea.
    (A) No sooner a turtle does
    (B) A turtle does no sooner
    (C) Does no sooner a turtle
    (D) No sooner does a turtle

11. _____ in medicine relieve distress but they also prevent and cure illness.
    (A) Not only do computers
    (B) Do computers
    (C) Computers
    (D) Computers not only

12. Not only _____ in the field of psychology but animal behavior is examined as well.
    (A) human behavior is studied
    (B) is human behavior studied
    (C) is studied human behavior
    (D) human behavior

CHAPTER 15
WORD FORMS

Introduction: Benjamin Franklin

Benjamin Franklin was an American politician, inventor, and scientist. He was born in 1706 and at the age of ten set to work in his father's candle and soap business. However, he disliked his work and two years later he went to work for a printer. He eventually became a successful printer, producing a weekly newspaper and popular books. He also became a politician and helped the United States become free from British rule. His inventions included a smokeless stove, bifocal lenses, and new types of fertilizer.

In 1752 Franklin conducted a dangerous experiment. By flying a kite during a storm, he discovered that a lightning bolt is just a large electric spark. Franklin put his discovery to use and invented the lightning conductor. This is a thick metal wire that ran from the top of a building to the ground. If lightning struck the building, the electricity would travel down the wire to the ground and therefore would not damage the building or harm the people inside. This discovery was the first step in developing ways of making use of electricity to power machines.

Exercise 1

> **Word forms are tested on the TOEFL® Test. Fill in the blanks with the correct words from the reading.**

1. Franklin was a famous politician and _____.

2. After working in his father's business, he worked for a _____.

3. Later he became a _____ and helped the United States become free from the British.

4. In 1752 Franklin did a _____ experiment by flying a kite in a storm.

5. A lightning conductor was a _____ _____ wire that ran from the top of a building to the ground.

6. What Franklin discovered during the storm was put to good _____ by his invention of the lightning conductor.

Exercise 2

> From the reading decide whether these statements are *true* or *false*.

1. Benjamin Franklin was not a success as a printer.   T F
2. Benjamin Franklin is famous only in politics and for his invention of fertilizers.   T F
3. Franklin's kite experiment in a storm was dangerous.   T F
4. The lightning conductor is a thick electric wire that runs from the top of a building to the ground.   T F
5. Franklin discovered that lightning is electricity.   T F
6. Franklin's discovery helped to develop ways of using electricity as a source of power.   T F

Grammar: Word Forms

It is important to know if a word is a noun, a verb, an adjective, or an adverb. This is one of the most common types of error tested in the Written Expression section. As many as twenty percent of the items in this part of the test may be word form problems. These errors involve using one part of speech for another—a noun instead of a verb, an adjective instead of an adverb, and so on.

The form of a word depends on its position in a sentence. Look at how the word *electricity* changes form.

Noun form: **Electricity** *traveled down the wire.*
Verb form: *Franklin was not* **electrocuted** *by lightning.*
Adjective form: *An* **electrical** *current ran down the wire.*
Adverb form: *The machine runs* **electrically.**

NOUNS

Nouns can be identified by their position and/or function in a sentence. Knowing noun endings (suffixes) will also help identify nouns.

> **Strategy**
>
> Remember the correct noun form for a field of study and the name of the person who practices in that field.

CHAPTER 15 WORD FORMS

NOUN ENDINGS FOR PEOPLE:
Connected with a place or thing:

-ian   politician
-ist   scientist

People who do things:

-ee   employee
-er   printer
-or   inventor

NOUNS CONNECTED WITH FIELDS OF STUDY:

-ogy   biology
-ic(s) politics
-ation administration
-y   chemistry
-ce   science

Exercise 3

Choose the correct word in parentheses.

1. Franklin was a (politics/politician).
2. Franklin was also an (invention/inventor).
3. Franklin is known in the field of (science/scientist).
4. Franklin became a successful (printer/printing).
5. In 1820 a Danish (physicist/physics) proved that electricity produced magnetism.
6. One scientist who helped modern (chemist/chemistry) was Antoine Lavoisier.

Other noun endings (suffixes) include:

-acy	-en	-in	-ling
-age	-ess	-ing	-ment
-ance/ence	-ful	-ion	-ness
-ant/ent	-hood	-ism	-ocracy
-ate	-ia	-ite	-ry(ary/ery)
-ation	-ide	-ty	-ship
-dom			-ster
			-ive
			-y/ie

> **Strategy**
>
> Remember the correct noun or verb ending. Avoid confusion between nouns and verbs.

VERBS

Verbs are used to show the action of the subject.

*Franklin **discovered** that lightning is electricity.*

Verb endings include:

-ate	circulate	-er	discover
-en	sharpen	-ify	electrify
-ing	developing	-ize	politicize
-ed	invented		

EXERCISE 4

> **Make verbs from the following words:**

1. active
2. thick
3. sympathy
4. regular
5. solid
6. light

EXERCISE 5

> **Look at the underlined verbs or nouns. If the word is not correct, write the correct form.**

1. In Franklin's time electricity was mainly used as a form of <u>entertain</u>.
2. Franklin wanted <u>free</u> for the United States from British rule.
3. Franklin <u>discovery</u> that lightning was electricity.
4. Franklin was the only man to <u>signature</u> all four key documents that helped to make the United States independent.

5. Besides his many activities in the <u>serve</u> of his country, he found time to be an inventor.
6. Franklin <u>development</u> the first pair of bifocal spectacles.

ADJECTIVES

Adjectives modify or describe nouns. They usually come before nouns or after the verb *to be*. Adjectives usually answer the question "What kind?"

Adjectives have only *one* form, which is used with both singular and plural nouns.

*Franklin was a **brave** scientist.*

Adjective endings include:

-al/ial	-ing
-able/ible	-ish
-ant/ent	-ive
-ary	-less
-ory	-like
-ed	-ly
-er	-some
-ful	-ous
-ic	-worthy
-ile	-y

> **Strategy**
>
> The most common type of word form error occurs when an adjective is used as an adverb or an adverb is used as an adjective. Keep in mind that an adjective answers the question "What kind?" and an adverb answers the question "How?" Look at the endings of adjectives and adverbs.

ADVERBS

Adverbs modify verbs, adverbs, and adjectives. Adverbs usually answer the question "How?" Adverbs are often formed by adding *-ly* to an adjective.

Adjective: brave
Adverb: bravely

Exceptions: The adverbs *hard, fast,* and *high* have the same form as adjectives.

Some adjectives end in *-ly* like adverbs: *friendly, costly, yearly*.

Adverb endings include:
-ly
-ward
-wise

Exercise 6

Choose the correct adjective or adverb in parentheses.

1. Franklin became a (successfully/successful) printer.
2. At age 40, Franklin became (interested/interestingly) in electricity.
3. Franklin produced a (week/weekly) newspaper and many popular books.
4. The lightning conductor attracted lightning and carried it (safe/safely) to the ground.
5. Among his many inventions was a (smokelessly/smokeless) stove.
6. Franklin put his invention to (well/good) use.

Exercise 7

Identify the following words as a *noun (N)*, a *verb (V)*, an *adjective (ADJ)*, or an *adverb (ADV)*.

1. dangerous _____
2. electricity _____
3. invention _____
4. scientist _____
5. successful _____
6. experiment _____
7. discovery _____
8. development _____
9. brilliantly _____
10. conductor _____

CHAPTER 15 WORD FORMS 139

Exercise 8

> **Identify the underlined word as a *noun* (N), a *verb* (V), an *adjective* (ADJ), or an *adverb* (ADV).**

1. Benjamin Franklin was <u>cautious</u> in performing his famous kite experiment.
2. The first two men who tried to repeat Franklin's experiment were <u>electrocuted</u>.
3. He flew a kite fitted with a <u>metal</u> key into a storm cloud.
4. Franklin <u>eventually</u> became a successful printer.
5. When <u>lightning</u> hit the key, sparks flew off it.
6. Franklin proved that storm clouds are <u>charged</u> with electricity.
7. Lightning is caused by the <u>discharge</u> of electricity in the form of a spark.
8. Franklin was able to prove that storm clouds have <u>static</u> electricity.

On the TOEFL® Test

In the Written Expression section, the most common errors tested are word form errors. Of these, the most frequent are the following:

1. The use of an adjective instead of an adverb or an adverb instead of an adjective.

    Example: Around 1750, <u>electricity</u> <u>experiments</u> became <u>popularly</u> as
                                    A   B   C
    <u>entertainment</u> at the court of the French King, Louis XV.
          D

    The best answer is (C). An adjective, *popular*, not an adverb, is required.

    Example: In 1780, Italian <u>scientist</u> Luigi Galvani <u>mistaken</u> concluded
                                   A   B
    that frogs' legs <u>contain</u> <u>electricity</u>.
                C   D

    The correct answer is (B). An adverb, *mistakenly*, is needed to modify the verb *concluded*.

2. The name of a field of study is mistakenly used for the person who practices it, or a field of study is confused with an adjective describing it.

   Example: As well as being underline{successful} in his many underline{careers}, Benjamin
                                      A   B
   Franklin was well-known as a science.
                     C   D

   The best answer is (D). *Science* is the name of the field. The correct answer is *scientist,* the name of the person who practices in the field.

3. Other word form errors include the use of incorrect forms for nouns, verbs, adjectives, and adverbs.

   Example: Electricity produced by nature is called static electricity
                                       A   B
   because it exerts a forceful when it is stationary.
                        C   D

   The best answer is (C). The noun *force,* not the adjective *forceful,* is needed.

   Example: When lightning strikes an unprotected building, the electric
                                          A   B
   charge can cause considering damage.
                  C   D

   The correct answer is (C). The adjective *considerable* is needed instead of the gerund *considering*.

EXERCISES ON WORD FORMS

> **From the four underlined words or phrases (A), (B), (C), or (D), identify the *one* that is not correct.**

1. Diamonds are graded according to weigh, color, and cut.
      A   B   C   D

2. As an educator, John Dewey opposed the traditional method of learning
           A   B
   by memory under the authorize of teachers.
      C   D

3. A substantial proportional of the printers and newspaper publishers in
        A   B   C
   colonial America were women.
      D

CHAPTER 15 WORD FORMS   141

4. Many seeds remain <u>dormantly</u> in the ground until conditions <u>involving</u>
                          A   B
   <u>heat</u> and water are correct for <u>germination</u>.
    C   D

5. Lavoisier was the first to recognize the <u>importance</u> of <u>accurately</u>
                                                     A   B
   measurements when studying <u>chemical</u> <u>changes</u>.
                                      C   D

6. Nails act as a <u>hard</u> base for the <u>sensitive</u> skin of the fingertips and toe
                    A   B
   tips to press against, so they may help our <u>sensitively</u> to <u>touch</u>.
                                                        C   D

7. Lichens can survive <u>extremes</u> of <u>heat</u>, <u>cold</u>, and <u>dry</u>.
                           A   B   C   D

8. Diamond is the <u>hardest</u> known mineral, <u>whereas</u> graphite is very <u>soft</u>
                A   B   C
   and <u>flake</u>.
       D

9. Medicine in the future will make increasing use of high <u>technology</u> for
    A   B
   the <u>investigate</u> and diagnosis of illnesses, as well as for their <u>treatment</u>.
         C   D

10. Herman Melville's work, which is <u>complexity</u>, <u>philosophical</u>, and
                                                    A   B
    <u>humorous</u>, is recognized as one of the most astonishing <u>achievements</u> in
       C   D
    all American literature.

11. Cells carry out the <u>essentially</u> <u>processes</u> that produce <u>energy</u> and <u>sustain</u>
                               A   B   C   D
    life.

12. Like their ancestors, most sharks are <u>streamline</u>, <u>fast-swimming</u> <u>hunters</u>
                                                  A   B   C
    living in the upper waters of <u>warm</u> seas.
                                         D

CHAPTER 16: WORD CHOICE AND REDUNDANCY

Introduction: Asbestos

Asbestos is a type of mineral found in rocks that has a fibrous structure and so can be woven. Unlike other flexible woven material, it is capable of withstanding very high temperatures, and at the same time deflecting heat. Woven metal wire, for example, might do the first job, but would not do the second. For this reason, asbestos gloves, suits, and shields have been vital for protection in fire fighting. There are hundreds of uses for asbestos in industry and construction. Asbestos can be mixed with other materials, such as rubber, graphite, paint, and cement, for special purposes that demand extra flexibility, slipperiness, coating quality, or hardness. Asbestos is so useful that it was once found in almost all modern buildings and machines. Modern industry has also benefited from its uses as a material for electrical and sound insulation.

    The unique properties of asbestos have led to its continued but restricted use. In this century, industries in the United States alone have used more than 30 million tons of asbestos. However, after 1950 health warnings about asbestos began to appear. Its small fibers, so useful in other respects, could also be inhaled and lodge in the lungs to cause a disease called asbestosis. This disease restricts normal breathing. Chronic shortness of breath turns sufferers into invalids. Worse still, there is also the risk that lung cancer may follow.

CHAPTER 16 WORD CHOICE AND REDUNDANCY

Exercise 1

> Word choice errors are tested on the TOEFL® Test. Complete the sentences by choosing the correct words from the reading.

1. Unlike/like other woven material, asbestos is capable of withstanding high temperature and at the same time deflecting heat.
2. Asbestos is such/so useful that it was once used in a lot of modern buildings.
3. After/afterwards 1950, health warnings about asbestos began to appear.
4. Previously asbestos was used in almost/most all modern buildings and machines.
5. Woven metal wire can withstand heat and/but cannot deflect heat.
6. There are hundreds of uses of asbestos in industry and/or construction.

Exercise 2

> A word can have the same meaning as another word, but two words with the same meaning cannot be used together. Match the words in the box with the words underlined in the sentences below.
>
> a. such as   b. chiefly   c. carefully
> d. beneficial e. single

1. Asbestos is <u>mainly</u> used in industry and construction.
2. Asbestos can be mixed with other materials, <u>for example</u>, rubber.
3. The small fibers of asbestos, so <u>useful</u> in other ways, could harm the body.
4. Asbestos has some <u>unique</u> qualities.
5. When removing asbestos today, it is important to handle it <u>cautiously</u>.

Grammar: Word Choice

A number of words in English often cause problems because they have similar meanings (make/do) or sound alike (alike/unlike). Many times one word is used incorrectly in place of another.

> **Strategy**
>
> Learn the expressions with *make* and *do*. Whenever you hear a new expression, add it to the list. In the Written Expression section of the test, whenever *make* or *do* is underlined, look for an error.

Make or Do

The verb *to make* means to produce or create, whereas *to do* means to perform, to act. These two verbs are found in a number of expressions.

Expressions with *make* include:

make a mistake	make a plan
make a difference	make an investment
make a comparison	make an offer
make a discovery	make a choice
make use of	make an attempt
make a profit	make a decision
make a suggestion	make a prediction

Expressions with *do* include:

do one's duty	do harm
do homework	do research
do justice to	do an assignment
do business	do one's best
do wrong	do a service
do work	do damage
do a kindness	do wonders

EXERCISE 3

> **Underline the word that correctly completes the sentence.**

1. A wide range of new products is now available to (do/make) many of the jobs once (done/made) by materials (made/done) with asbestos.

2. Modern products (made/done) with asbestos look different from the ones that caused problems in the past.

CHAPTER 16 WORD CHOICE AND REDUNDANCY

3. Usually radon disperses in the open air and would (do/make) no harm to your body.
4. When radium was mixed with other substances it (made/did) them luminous.
5. Marie Curie (made/did) a great contribution to science through her discovery of radium, although it proved fatal to her.
6. A distinction has been (made/done) between the dangers of blue and white asbestos.

LIKE/ALIKE/UNLIKE

> **Strategy**
> Look for the different parts of speech of the words *like/alike/unlike* as well as their different meanings to avoid confusion.

Like is a preposition that means "similar." It is followed by an object.

> **Like** many other people, I did not know the dangers of asbestos.

Alike is an adverb that means "equally"; as an adjective, it means "similar."

> The new information on asbestos caused panic in construction and industry **alike**.

Unlike is a preposition that means "not similar." It is followed by an object.

> **Unlike** other woven material, asbestos is capable of withstanding high temperatures and at the same time deflecting heat.

EXERCISE 4

> **Underline the word that correctly completes the sentence.**

1. (Unlike/Alike) blue asbestos, white asbestos is safe when its fibers are sealed off and left undisturbed.
2. Both blue and brown asbestos are (alike/like) in that they are both dangerous.
3. (Like/Alike) all metals, alkaline-earth metals conduct heat and electricity well.
4. Radon, (like/alike) radium, is radioactive.

5. Today synthetic plastic foam is used for insulation, but (unlike/alike) asbestos it cannot be used where there are high temperatures.

6. Asbestos and radium are (alike/like) in that they are both dangerous.

OTHER/THE OTHER/ANOTHER

Another means "one more." It can be used before a singular noun.

    We need to find **another** way.

Other means "more of the ones in the group we are talking about." It is used before a plural noun.

    Asbestos protects **other** materials from fire.

The other means "the last one of the group we are talking about." It is used before a singular noun, or a noncount noun. It is preceded by a determiner such as *the, some, any, no,* or *one.*

    No other material is capable of withstanding such temperature.

    One type of asbestos is dangerous; **the other** type is not as dangerous.

EXERCISE 5

> **Circle the word that correctly completes the sentence.**

1. Another/Other airy material is glass fiber.

2. Ancient Egyptians used asbestos to weave funeral garments for kings and other/another important people.

3. White asbestos, or chyrsolite, is another/other kind of asbestos.

4. Asbestos can be mixed with another/other materials such as rubber, paint, and cement.

5. Other/Another products are now available to do jobs where asbestos was once used.

6. Besides being a good heat and electrical insulator, other/the other use of asbestos has been to keep down noise levels in public buildings.

SO/SUCH/TOO

Both *so . . . that* and *such . . . that* have the same meaning, but they are used with different constructions. *So . . . that* is used with *many, few, much,* and *little*.

> *so* + adverb/adjective + *that*
>
> Asbestos was **so convenient that** everybody used it.
>
> *such* + adjective + noun + *that*
>
> Asbestos had **such unique qualities that** it was used widely.

Too means more than necessary. It comes before an adjective or adverb and is followed by an infinitive.

> Asbestos is **too dangerous** to be used widely.

EXERCISE 6

> **Circle the word that correctly completes the sentence.**

1. Asbestos has such/so many properties that it was used in all modern buildings.
2. Asbestos is so/such dangerous that it has been banned in many countries.
3. Asbestos is considered to be so/too dangerous to be used in buildings today.
4. Asbestos was so/too widely used in construction that it is creating problems today.
5. Asbestos can stand such/too high temperatures that it was used as protective clothing by fire fighters.
6. Asbestos is too/so dangerous to be removed without wearing protective clothing or gloves.

MUCH/MANY/FEW/LITTLE

Many and *few* are used with count nouns.

> **Example:** *Many old buildings have asbestos.*

Much and *little* are used with noncount nouns.

> **Example:** *There is **much** caution when dealing with the material today.*

EXERCISE 7

> **Circle the word that correctly completes the sentence.**

1. Much/Many blue asbestos is mined in South Africa, Bolivia, and Australia.
2. A small amount of radiation can help cure someone, whereas too much/many will cause harm.
3. Madame Curie, after many/much years of exposure to radium, died of anemia.
4. A little/few radon can be found in much/many types of soil.
5. Few/Little people have had the bad luck to live in an area with a high natural background level of radiation.
6. There was little/few information about the dangers of asbestos before the 1950s.

OTHER COMMONLY CONFUSED WORDS

> **Strategy**
> Other words may also be used in word choice errors. The most common words used on the test are listed below. Learn the difference between the words in pairs by looking them up in the dictionary to find out what parts of speech they are and the difference in meaning.

The following words may also be used in word choice problems.

number/amount	near/nearly
few/a few	after/afterward
little/a little	no/not
because/because of	and/but/or
despite/in spite of/although	most/almost
percent/percentage	ago/before
hard/hardly	age/old
twice/double	either . . . or/neither . . . nor
some/somewhat	person/people

CHAPTER 16 WORD CHOICE AND REDUNDANCY

Exercise 8

> **Circle the word that correctly completes the sentence.**

1. An amount/A number of contaminated buildings are known to release dangerous amounts of radioactivity over a period of years.

2. Because of/Although its danger to health, asbestos has been banned in many countries.

3. Synthetic plastic foam should no/not be used where there are high temperatures or any risk of fire.

4. Afterward/After the danger of asbestos was known, glass fiber began to be used widely for heat insulation.

5. Radon is radioactive, and it decays to produce some/somewhat very unhealthy properties.

6. Radon gas is not a threat to human life almost/most of the time.

Grammar: Redundancy

Redundancy is the unnecessary repetition of an idea.
   Correct: The party proceeded toward the west.
   Redundant: The party proceeded forward toward the west.
The word *proceeded* has the same meaning as *forward*. Therefore, the word *forward* is unnecessary.

   The following pairs of words have the same meaning; only one in the pair is necessary.

connect	together	incorrect	mistake
repeat	again	important	significant
join	together	carefully	cautiously
proceed	forward	established	founded
progress	forward	protect	guard
advance	forward	original	first
only	unique	rarely	seldom
new	innovations	transmit	send out
reread	again	single	only
return	back	around	approximately
same	identical	chief	main
sufficient	enough	such as	for example
separated	apart from	necessary	needed

Exercise 9

> **Circle the number of each sentence that contains a redundant expression.**

1. Asbestos can be mixed with other materials, for example such as rubber, paint, and cement.

2. Because asbestos does not burn and only melts at high temperatures, it can protect and guard other material against fire.

3. One of the main and chief uses of asbestos is to weave gloves, aprons, and other clothing for workers in hot places such as metal foundries.

4. When asbestos fibers are breathed in or swallowed, they can cause serious disease, even cancer.

5. Asbestos shields off, or insulates against, heat, flames, electricity, and noise.

6. The unique and single properties of asbestos mean that it has many important uses.

7. No new innovations have been developed to replace asbestos being used for brake linings on cars.

8. For around approximately thirty years, only white asbestos has been used for protective clothing because it is safer than other forms of asbestos.

On the TOEFL® Test

Word choice errors that involve the incorrect use of one word for another appear in the Written Expression section. The words given in this chapter are frequently used in word choice errors. The following are some of the most common errors:

1. Wrong use of *so . . . that, such . . . that,* and *too:*

    Example: Asbestos is so a useful material that it was used in almost all
                          A   B   C D
    modern buildings.

    The best choice is (B); the correct construction is *such* + adjective + noun + *that* clause.

CHAPTER 16 WORD CHOICE AND REDUNDANCY   151

2. Wrong use of *another, other, the other:*

   Example: Other, more common, name for crocidolite is blue asbestos
                  A   B
   because of its color.
        C   D

   The best answer is (A); *other* is used incorrectly instead of *another*.

3. Wrong use of *make* and *do*

   Example: When asbestos fibers are breathed in, they may make damage
             A   B   C
   to our lungs.
   D

   The best choice is (C); the expression is *do damage* and not *make damage*.

EXERCISES ON WORD CHOICE AND REDUNDANCY

> **From the four underlined words or phrases, (A), (B), (C), or (D), identify the *one* that is not correct.**

1. About 200 million years before all the continents were part of one vast
         A   B   C   D
   land mass called Pangaea.

2. Investment banks do not accept deposits from the public or do loans to
        A   B   C
   businesses or individuals.
   D

3. White blood cells live only for a little days because they are poisoned by
                      A   B   C
   the bacteria they capture.
                     D

4. When actively hunting, a dolphin sends out transmitting about five
      A   B   C
   signals every second.
          D

5. A mainframe computer is large and is usually used to operate a network
                                    A   B   C
   of another computers.
      D

6. So far most a million different species of insects have been identified
   —A— —B—   —C—   —D—
   and named.

7. The sun contains 99.9 percentage of the mass of the solar system.
              —A—   —B—   —C— —D—

8. Lewis and Clark had been gone for such long on their expedition that
                      —A—   —B—
   many thought they were dead.
   —C—   —D—

9. A living polyp looks like little sea anemone, with tentacles to trap tiny
     —A—   —B—   —C—
   animals for food.
           —D—

10. The giant panda eats chiefly mainly bamboo shoots, though it also eats
                            —A—   —B—
    some other plants and occasionally feeds on fish and small rodents.
         —C—   —D—

11. Most of the Egyptian woman Hypatia's writings on medicine have been
    —A—
    lost, but there are an amount of references to them by other scientists.
         —B—   —C—   —D—

12. Alike most frogs, the clawed frog catches its prey with its hands.
    —A— —B—   —C—   —D—

PART II

Structure and Written Expression Practice Tests

PRACTICE TEST 1

Directions

Items in the first part of this section are incomplete sentences. Under each of these sentences, there are four words or phrases. You will choose the **one** word or phrase—(A), (B), (C), or (D)—that best completes the sentence.

EXAMPLE I

Reflexes _____ very valuable in protecting the body against harm.

- (A) that are
- (B) being
- (C) are
- (D) are being

The sentence should read, "Reflexes are very valuable in protecting the body against harm." You should therefore choose (C).

EXAMPLE II

Seismographs are used to locate oil, to determine ocean depth, and _____ and measure earthquakes.

- (A) detect
- (B) to detect
- (C) be detecting
- (D) are detecting

The sentence should read, "Seismographs are used to locate oil, to determine ocean depth, and to detect and measure earthquakes." You should therefore choose (B).

1. Snakes have an organ in a pit on their heads _____ infrared rays.
   (A) detects
   (B) a detection of
   (C) it detects
   (D) that detects

2. Helium is not inflammable, _____ therefore safer than hydrogen.
   (A) that is
   (B) and is
   (C) but is
   (D) and it

3. In 1849 Walter Hunt, _____ American inventor, patented a design that served as the basis for modern safety pins.
   (A) an
   (B) he was an
   (C) being
   (D) who was, as an

4. Ansel Adams was a landscape photographer _____ photographs of the western United States show nature on a grand scale.
   (A) whose
   (B) of his
   (C) of whom
   (D) his

5. Contact lenses _____ of acrylic are more transparent and less fragile than lenses made of glass.
   (A) making
   (B) made
   (C) are made
   (D) which make

6. _____ other cells in the body, nerve cells are not healed or replaced when they are damaged or destroyed.
   (A) Different
   (B) Unlikely
   (C) Unlike
   (D) But

7. The higher the content of carbon dioxide in the air, _____.
   (A) more heat it retains
   (B) than it retains more heat
   (C) it retains more heat
   (D) the more heat it retains

8. _____ most brilliant Greek inventor was Archimedes, who lived about 2,250 years ago.
   (A) The
   (B) One of the
   (C) As the
   (D) Of the

9. _____ flying, a bat emits a rapid series of ultrasonic signals, which bounce off any object in its path.
   (A) When it
   (B) When it is
   (C) It is
   (D) When is

10. _____ does not circle around the earth was proven by Galileo.
    (A) Since the rest of the universe
    (B) As the rest of the universe
    (C) The rest of the universe
    (D) That the rest of the universe

11. _____ cell in the body is far from a capillary.
    (A) Not
    (B) No
    (C) Not only a
    (D) Neither a

12. Ralph Waldo Emerson's belief _____ the individual freedom of all people greatly influenced later American thinkers.
    (A) as of
    (B) on
    (C) in
    (D) as in

13. Thomas Malthus claimed that disease, war, famine, and _____ act as checks on population growth.
    (A) moral restraining
    (B) morally restrain
    (C) by moral restraint
    (D) moral restraint

14. _____ phobias do not involve loss of contact with reality, they may severely limit a person's life.
    (A) Although
    (B) Despite
    (C) That
    (D) As

15. During the 1930s, unsuitable farming techniques and excessive grazing of grassland in the Great Plains produced _____.
    (A) which it became known as the Dust Bowl
    (B) what became known as the Dust Bowl
    (C) it became known as the Dust Bowl
    (D) that it became known as the Dust Bowl

PRACTICE TEST 1

> **Directions**
>
> The rest of the items in this section consist of sentences in which four words or phrases have been underlined.
>
> You must identify the **one** underlined expression—(A), (B), (C), or (D)—that must be changed in order to correct the sentence.

Example I

Navajo Indians are far more numerous today as they were in the past.
     A   B   C   D

    The sentence should read, "Navajo Indians are far more numerous today than they were in the past." You should therefore choose answer (C).

    Though it is one of the rarest metals, gold was one of the first to be
        A   B   C
discover.
D

    The sentence should read, "Though it is one of the rarest metals, gold was one of the first to be discovered." You should therefore choose answer (D).

16. The first laser is made by an American scientist called Theodore Maiman
          A   B   C
    working in California in 1960.
    D

17. Almost medical doctors have had some training in psychology and
    A   B   C D
    psychiatry.

18. Washington Irving, one of America's most famous authors, was a lawyer,
                                                 A   B
    a businessman, and a United States diplomatic to England and Spain.
                            C   D

19. The Douglas fir is a very tall American evergreen tree that is grown not
                                                                A
    only for ornament and for its high-quality timber.
           B   C   D

20. Nuclear energy, a almost limitless source of power, was harnessed
              A   B   C
    during the mid-1900s.
           D

21. Plants, which <u>make up</u> 90 <u>percentage</u> of visible <u>living</u> organisms, get
             A   B   C
    their <u>food</u> energy from sunlight.
          D

22. <u>Total</u> eclipses of the moon <u>are</u> <u>considerably</u> <u>rarest</u> than total eclipses of
     A   B   C   D
    the sun.

23. <u>According to</u> Freud, mental life is <u>characterized</u> by internal conflicts <u>who</u>
         A   B   C
    are <u>largely</u> unconscious.
        D

24. In 1729, Benjamin Franklin <u>published</u> the *Pennsylvania Gazette,* <u>which</u>
                                A   D
    soon became the most <u>read widely</u> newspaper in the colonies.
         C   D

25. Large, <u>perfect</u> shaped pearls rank <u>in</u> value with <u>the</u> most <u>precious</u>
            A   B   C   D
    stones.

26. Algae range <u>in</u> size from <u>microscope</u> <u>one-celled</u> plants to huge <u>masses</u> of
                A   B   C   D
    seaweed.

27. <u>The</u> pharmacology is a recent science, but it is <u>closely</u> connected with
     A   B
    one of the oldest, <u>the</u> giving of <u>remedies</u> to relieve diseases.
                         C   D

28. Frances Perkins, <u>the</u> first woman to become <u>a</u> U.S. cabinet member, was
                      A   B
    <u>instrument</u> in the <u>adoption</u> of the Social Security Act.
        C   D

29. In <u>the company</u> of human beings, parrots demonstrate a <u>remarkable</u>
          A   B
    talent <u>for</u> mimicry, <u>for which</u> they never use in the forest.
           C   D

30. The first <u>national</u> known male singers <u>of</u> popular music <u>appeared</u> during
              A   B   C   D
    the 1920s.

31. The Puffer is <u>a</u> type of fish <u>that</u> can inflate <u>one's</u> body <u>like</u> a balloon.
                  A   B   C   D

32. The Louisiana Purchase, made in 1803, almost was doubled the size of
             A   B   C   D
    the United States.

33. Psychology did not develop into a science based of careful observation
                                     A   B   C
    and experimentation until the late 1800s.
        D

34. When a mineral forms, it grows by the addition of various element to its
     A   B   C   D
    structure.

35. Energy exists in different forms, such as light, heat, and chemical,
                   A   B
    mechanic, and electrical energy.
      C   D

36. Modern art began in second half of the 1800s, after the camera was
                         A   B   C   D
    invented.

37. Although polar bears hunt other animals, they seldom rarely kill people.
      A   B   C   D

38. Mushrooms get their food by causing vegetable matter decaying.
                   A   B   C   D

39. Limestone long has been quarried for to use as a building stone.
               A   B   C   D

40. The newborn marsupial is at a least developed stage of life than a
                             A   B   C
    newborn kitten or human being.
                   D

PRACTICE TEST 2

Directions

Items in the first part of this section are incomplete sentences. Under each of these sentences, there are four words or phrases. You will choose the **one** word or phrase—(A), (B), (C), or (D)—that best completes the sentence.

EXAMPLE I

Reflexes _____ very valuable in protecting the body against harm.

- **(A)** that are
- **(B)** being
- **(C)** are
- **(D)** are being

The sentence should read, "Reflexes are very valuable in protecting the body against harm." You should therefore choose (C).

EXAMPLE II

Seismographs are used to locate oil, to determine ocean depth, and _____ and measure earthquakes.

- **(A)** detect
- **(B)** to detect
- **(C)** be detecting
- **(D)** are detecting

The sentence should read, "Seismographs are used to locate oil, to determine ocean depth, and to detect and measure earthquakes." You should therefore choose (B).

1. The core of the moon is much smaller, in relation to its size, _____ of the planets
   - (A) those
   - (B) than those
   - (C) ones
   - (D) than are those

2. Silver is sometimes mixed with copper _____ an alloy that is harder and stronger than pure silver.
   - (A) to form
   - (B) forms
   - (C) it forms
   - (D) the forming of

3. Samuel Clemens, _____ under the pen name Mark Twain, created characters that reflected purely American traits and habits.
   - (A) he wrote
   - (B) and he wrote
   - (C) who wrote
   - (D) wrote

4. _____ beetles have hard wing cases that protect the wings when not in use.
   - (A) Of all
   - (B) All
   - (C) Because all
   - (D) They are all

5. Not _____ anywhere in the thirteen colonies before the American Revolution.
   - (A) a single bank
   - (B) a bank existed single
   - (C) existed a single bank
   - (D) a single bank existed

6. _____ mosquito bites a human being or other animal suffering from a certain disease, it carries off the disease germs in its saliva.
   - (A) A
   - (B) Should a
   - (C) Whenever a
   - (D) That a

7. _____ in 1607, Jamestown in Virginia was the first settlement in the New World.
   - (A) Founded
   - (B) It was founded
   - (C) Founding
   - (D) To be found

8. Both the lantern fish and the deep sea angler _____ a luminous gland system in their bodies.
   - (A) they have
   - (B) have
   - (C) had
   - (D) having

9. An effective paragraph must _____ be unified and ordered but also complete.
   - (A) in addition
   - (B) either
   - (C) not only
   - (D) as well

10. _____, the Mormons fled from Illinois in 1846.
    - (A) Their religious beliefs made
    - (B) Their religious beliefs because
    - (C) Because their beliefs, religious
    - (D) Because of their religious beliefs

11. Aristotle, _____ the greatest of the Greek philosophers, wrote extensively about physics and other sciences.
    (A) one of
    (B) he is one of
    (C) of
    (D) it is he one of

12. Exactly _____ we can replace our soil disappearing through erosion is not known.
    (A) what
    (B) how
    (C) if
    (D) by which

13. _____ varieties of potato that produce three-quarters of the U.S. potato crop.
    (A) There are four
    (B) They are four
    (C) Four of the
    (D) Of the four

14. Henry Ford, _____, was an outstanding innovator.
    (A) he founded the Ford Motor Company
    (B) founded the Ford Motor Company
    (C) who founded the Ford Motor Company
    (D) the Ford Motor Company founded

15. Pheasants spend most of their time on the ground, _____ many species perch in trees at night.
    (A) as well as
    (B) in spite of
    (C) because
    (D) although

Directions

The rest of the items in this section consist of sentences in which four words or phrases have been underlined. You must identify the **one** underlined expression—(A), (B), (C), or (D)—that must be changed in order to correct the sentence.

EXAMPLE I

Navajo Indians are far more numerous today as they were in the past.
     A   B   C   D

    The sentence should read, "Navajo Indians are far more numerous today than they were in the past." You should therefore choose answer (C).

    Though it is one of the rarest metals, gold was one of the first to be
       A   B   C
discover.
D

    The sentence should read, "Though it is one of the rarest metals, gold was one of the first to be discovered." You should therefore choose answer (D).

    Though it is one of the rarest metals, gold was one of the first to be
       A   B   C
discover.
D

    The sentence should read, "Though it is one of the rarest metals, gold was one of the first to be discovered." You should therefore choose answer (D).

16. Wind erodes the land by picking up grains of sand and hurling it against
     A   B   C   D
rocks.

17. The Kodak was the first camera designed specifically for both mass
                A   B   C
production or amateur use.
          D

18. Phlebitis, an inflammation of a vein, can develop in any part of the body,
                                     A   B
but it most commonly occurs in their legs.
        C   D

19. Certain bacteria can capture light energy and uses it to make food.
       A   B   C   D

20. During the 1850s and 1860s many people began to experiment with the
         A   B   C
    artist possibilities of photography.
      D

21. Aristotle believed that the mind or soul, who the Greeks called psyche,
                           A   B
    was separate from the body.
         C   D

22. The earth is the only planet with a large number of oxygen in its
              A   B   C   D
    atmosphere.

23. The exciting, naturally, free movement of modern dance began with
      A   B   C   D
    Isadora Duncan.

24. Albany, a city on the Hudson River, was the capital of New York State
           A   B   C D
    since 1797.

25. Birds have a poor sense of smell but very good hearings and eyesight.
      A   B   C   D

26. Placebos look like real drugs, but most consist only in sugar or a salt
         A   B C   D
    solution.

27. The Pueblo Indians have traditionally live in stone or adobe structures
                  A   B   C
    that resemble apartment buildings.
     D

28. Fabrics woven from plastic fibers feel soft, but the fibers are make from
         A   B   C
    hard plastics.
        D

29. In about 1960, chemists have developed synthetic pheromones that are
        A   B   C
    used to control insect pests.
                  D

30. The spinal cord is the main pathway for messages traveling between the
                A   B   C
    brain to the rest of the body.
        D

31. After Yellowstone National Park was set up in 1871 as the first National
                                     ———————   ———
                                        A   B
    Park, another national parks have been established throughout the
          ———————   ——————————
             C   D
    world.

32. Nearly all chemical agents are harmful to living tissue if enough of them
    ———   ——————————   ————
      A   B   C
    is taken.
    ————————
       D

33. In 1875, the American philosopher William James founded what was
                                                    ——————— ————
                                                       A   B
    probable the world's first psychology laboratory.
    ————————   ——————————
        C   D

34. Few natural prairie regions remain in the world because of most of them
                                —————   ————————   ————
                                  A   B   C
    have been turned into farms or grazing land.
                    ————
                      D

35. Most species of pigeons live in flocks, and many of the flocks consist
                    ——————— ————   ———————
                       A   B   C
    more than one species.
             ———————————
                  D

36. Astronomers do not think are there any planets in the solar system
    ———————————   ————— ——— ————— ———
          A   B   C   D
    beyond Pluto.

37. When an enemy scares a porcupine fish, it enters a hole in a rock and
                  ——————   ——————
                    A   B
    to fill its stomach with water to make its spines stick out.
    ——————   ———
       C   D

38. Robert Frost was not well known as a poet until he reached the forties.
                                     ——— ——————   ——————— ———
                                      A   B   C   D

39. Mushrooms get their food by to cause vegetable matter to decay.
              ——— ————— ———— ————————— ——————————————
               A   B   C   D

40. The pharynx plays an important significant role in speech, especially in
    ———   ———————————   ——————————— ——
     A   B   C   D
    the production of vowel sounds.

PRACTICE TEST 3

Directions

Items in the first part of this section are incomplete sentences. Under each of these sentences, there are four words or phrases. You will choose the **one** word or phrase—(A), (B), (C), or (D)—that best completes the sentence.

EXAMPLE I

Reflexes _____ very valuable in protecting the body against harm.

    (A) that are
    (B) being
    (C) are
    (D) are being

The sentence should read, "Reflexes are very valuable in protecting the body against harm." You should therefore choose (C).

EXAMPLE II

Seismographs are used to locate oil, to determine ocean depth, and _____ and measure earthquakes.

    (A) detect
    (B) to detect
    (C) be detecting
    (D) are detecting

The sentence should read, "Seismographs are used to locate oil, to determine ocean depth, and to detect and measure earthquakes." You should therefore choose (B).

1. Dow Jones and Company, _____, computes averages for each trading hour of every business day.
   (A) a financial publishing firm
   (B) is a financial publishing firm
   (C) that is a financial publishing firm
   (D) it is a financial publishing firm

2. _____ pipelines are expensive to build, they are relatively cheap to operate and maintain.
   (A) Because
   (B) That
   (C) Although
   (D) Despite

3. The pulse rate of children is faster _____ healthy adult.
   (A) the average
   (B) than that of the average
   (C) that of the average
   (D) as that of the average

4. During the 1970s, Thomas G. Stockham, Jr., a U.S. electrical engineer, _____ digital recording.
   (A) he developed
   (B) that developed
   (C) that he has developed
   (D) developed

5. In 1850 _____ established one of the first detective agencies in the United States.
   (A) detective Allan Pinkerton
   (B) it was detective Allan Pinkerton
   (C) detective Allan Pinkerton who
   (D) when detective Allan Pinkerton

6. _____, scientists have greatly increased the yield of crops such as corn, rice, and wheat.
   (A) As using the laws of genetics
   (B) Using the laws of genetics
   (C) The laws of genetics
   (D) The laws of genetics are to be used

7. _____, and they are separated from one another by vast distances.
   (A) Being millions of galaxies
   (B) Are millions of galaxies
   (C) Of the millions of galaxies
   (D) There are millions of galaxies

8. In 1776 Thomas Paine's popular and influential pamphlet *Common Sense* _____ the American colonists to declare their independence from English rule.
   (A) urged
   (B) to urge
   (C) to be urged
   (D) that urged

9. Artificial satellites provide data on atmospheric temperatures, solar radiation, and _____ the earth's surface.
   (A) reflect
   (B) reflecting
   (C) the reflection of
   (D) can reflect

10. The United States leads the world in the production of plastics, _____ about half the total output.
    (A) it supplies
    (B) supplying
    (C) to supply
    (D) supplies

11. _____ affect a person's body has long been known by doctors.
    (A) That emotional disturbances
    (B) Emotional disturbances
    (C) As emotional disturbances
    (D) If emotional disturbances

12. Regarded as one of the greatest physicists, _____.
    (A) the relationship between force and motion was first expressed by Isaac Newton
    (B) the first to express the relationship between force and motion was Isaac Newton
    (C) Isaac Newton was the first to express the relationship between force and motion
    (D) it was Isaac Newton who was the first to express the relationship between force and motion

13. When direct-dial telephones achieved _____ in the 1960s, nationwide faxing became possible.
    (A) used widespread
    (B) were used widespread
    (C) being used widespread
    (D) widespread use

14. Willa Cather, _____ a prominent American writer, grew up in Nebraska during the early farming years.
    (A) who became
    (B) became
    (C) she became
    (D) it is she who became

15. _____ few species that live on the ground, most monkeys live in trees.
    (A) There are
    (B) A
    (C) All but
    (D) Except for a

Directions

The rest of the items in this section consist of sentences in which four words or phrases have been underlined. You must identify the *one* underlined expression—(A), (B), (C), or (D)—that must be changed in order to correct the sentence.

EXAMPLE I

<u>Navajo Indians</u> are <u>far</u> more numerous today <u>as</u> they were <u>in</u> the past.
     A   B   C   D

    The sentence should read, "Navajo Indians are far more numerous today than they were in the past." You should therefore choose answer (C).

<u>Though</u> it is one of the rarest <u>metals</u>, gold was one of <u>the</u> first to be
  A   B   C
<u>discover</u>.
  D

    The sentence should read, "Though it is one of the rarest metals, gold was one of the first to be discovered." You should therefore choose answer (D).

16. <u>A</u> Geiger counter is an <u>electronic</u> instrument <u>is used</u> to measure the
      A   B   C
    presence and <u>intensity</u> of radiation.
                          D

17. <u>Warning</u> coloration protects a skunk by reminding <u>the</u> animal's enemies
       A   B
    of <u>their</u> ability to spray a
        C
    <u>foul-smelling</u> liquid.
        D

18. Natural gas was <u>probably</u> formed <u>from</u> plants and animals <u>that</u> decayed
                         A   B   C
    <u>million</u> of years ago.
      D

19. Three months after they have been <u>laid</u>, crocodile eggs are <u>ready</u>
                                             A   B   C
    <u>hatched</u>.
      D

20. The terrain of Antarctica, near one and a half times as big as the United
                    A   B   C
    States, is amazingly varied.
                D

21. Peas require rich soil, constant moistures, and a cool growing season to
                 A   B   C
    develop well.
            D

22. The amount of pectin in a fruit depends the species and ripeness.
        A   B   C   D

23. Most pageants are plays of special significant such as a drama portraying
    A   B   C   D
    the growth of a city or the development of medicine.

24. Joseph Priestley is immortal in the history of chemistry as the discover
                        A   B   C   D
    of oxygen, in 1774.

25. Mosses are useful in nature because of they are among the first plants to
                      A   B   C   D
    grow in barren lands.

26. Dreaming sleep may play a role in restoring the brain's ability to handle
    A   B
    such tasks as focused attention, memorize, and learning.
                  C   D

27. The most desert animals avoid the extreme midday heat by feeding at
        A   B   C   D
    night.

28. Although fewer Americans work on farms today, they are too productive
    A   B   C
    that the U.S. is now the world's top food exporter.
                                     D

29. Seals, turtles, and seabirds can navigate over thousands of miles of open
                                            A   B
    ocean with amazing accurate.
               C   D

30. Most mollusks have a hard shell that is protected their soft bodies.
                       A   B   C   D

31. Foods of animal origin generally supply greatest amounts of iron to the
                                     A   B   C   D
    diet than do foods of plant origin.

32. A dolphin locates underwater objects <u>in</u> <u>its</u> path by <u>doing</u> a series of
                                                  A B   C
    clicking and <u>whistling</u> sounds.
                    D

33. <u>In 1829</u>, James Smithson <u>set aside</u> money for <u>creating</u> of <u>the</u> Smithsonian
        A   B   C   D
    Institute.

34. <u>A</u> pheromone is a chemical substance released by <u>many</u> kinds of animals
    A   B
    to communicate with <u>another</u> members of <u>their</u> species.
                            C   D

35. The skin receives <u>nearly</u> <u>the</u> third of the blood <u>pumped out</u> <u>by</u> the heart.
                          A   B   C   D

36. <u>Alike</u> <u>most</u> small bats that fly by night, the large flying foxes <u>fly</u> <u>by</u> day.
    A   B   C D

37. Recognition <u>for</u> Herman Melville <u>did not come</u> <u>until</u> more than thirty
                   A   B   C
    years <u>afterward</u> his death in 1891.
              D

38. The Dewey system <u>is</u> widely used by libraries <u>throughout</u> the world; the
                           A   B
    <u>classification</u> <u>be</u> constantly revised.
        C   D

39. <u>Ten percent</u> of blood plasma is made up <u>mainly</u> <u>of</u> blood proteins which
        A   B C
    enable <u>itself</u> to clot.
          D

40. The American <u>frontiersman</u>, politician, and soldier Davy Crockett is one
                          A
    of the <u>most</u> popular <u>of</u> American <u>hero</u>.
         B   C   D

PRACTICE TEST 4

Directions

Items in the first part of this section are incomplete sentences. Under each of these sentences, there are four words or phrases. You will choose the *one* word or phrase—(A), (B), (C), or (D)—that best completes the sentence.

EXAMPLE I

Reflexes _____ very valuable in protecting the body against harm.

  (A) that are
  (B) being
  (C) are
  (D) are being

The sentence should read, "Reflexes are very valuable in protecting the body against harm." You should therefore choose (C).

EXAMPLE II

Seismographs are used to locate oil, to determine ocean depth, and _____ and measure earthquakes.

  (A) detect
  (B) to detect
  (C) be detecting
  (D) are detecting

The sentence should read, "Seismographs are used to locate oil, to determine ocean depth, and to detect and measure earthquakes." You should therefore choose (B).

1. Blood in vessels just under the nasal lining _____ up its heat to warm the air.
   (A) gives
   (B) it gives
   (C) giving
   (D) is given

2. The shuttle, _____ reusable spacecraft, lifts off like a rocket and lands like an airplane.
   (A) it is a
   (B) a
   (C) which, as a
   (D) is a

3. _____ forms of life, the most varied are the insects.
   (A) All are
   (B) All
   (C) They are all
   (D) Of all

4. The first American _____ a professional sculptor was a woman, Patience Lovell Wright.
   (A) she became as
   (B) became
   (C) to become
   (D) who she became

5. Tears not only _____ foreign substances from the eyes, but also contain chemicals that fight many common pathogens.
   (A) for washing
   (B) are washing
   (C) washing
   (D) wash

6. Carbonated beverages became popular in 1832 after _____ an apparatus for charging water with carbon dioxide gas.
   (A) invented John Mathews
   (B) John Mathews invented
   (C) inventing John Mathews
   (D) John Mathews inventing

7. The Pawnee Indians regarded corn _____ sacred gift, and many of their religious ceremonies are centered around this crop.
   (A) as being
   (B) since a
   (C) as a
   (D) like being

8. On Jupiter the winds have created storms _____ big that astronomers on Earth can see them through their telescopes.
   (A) so
   (B) such
   (C) as
   (D) how

9. Larger animals _____ than smaller animals of the same type.
   (A) longer live generally
   (B) they generally live long
   (C) generally live longer
   (D) live generally long

10. The tails of comets generally point away from the sun _____ the comet is approaching the sun or receding.
    (A) either
    (B) whether
    (C) and if
    (D) both

11. A desert is described as a region _____ an average of less than ten inches of rain falls in a year.
    (A) there is
    (B) which has
    (C) in which is
    (D) in which

12. Regular radio broadcasting to inform and entertain the general public _____ in the 1920s.
    (A) started
    (B) starting
    (C) a start
    (D) to start

13. _____ was made of minute particles called corpuscles was believed by scientists.
    (A) Light
    (B) That light
    (C) As light
    (D) Whereas light

14. _____ rain at all falls in the dry season in the savanna regions of Africa.
    (A) Not
    (B) Without
    (C) No
    (D) Neither

15. In a Rorschach test, the subject describes _____ sees in a series of inkblots.
    (A) that he or she
    (B) he or she
    (C) seeing he or she
    (D) what he or she

Directions

The rest of the items in this section consist of sentences in which four words or phrases have been underlined. You must identify the *one* underlined expression—(A), (B), (C), or (D)—that must be changed in order to correct the sentence.

Example I

Navajo Indians are far more numerous today as they were in the past.
      A   B   C   D

The sentence should read, "Navajo Indians are far more numerous today than they were in the past." You should therefore choose answer (C).

Though it is one of the rarest metals, gold was one of the first to be discover.
  A   B   C
D

The sentence should read, "Though it is one of the rarest metals, gold was one of the first to be discovered." You should therefore choose answer (D).

16. Pigeons, like many migratory birds, read the positions of
            A   B
the sun and stars in order to orient them.
         C   D

17. The cracking of rocks is caused of intense heat during the day followed
            A   B
by rapid cooling at night.
  C   D

18. Our nervous system has over ten billions nerve cells in a network
                               A   B
covering every inch of our skin and organs.
      C   D

19. Great quantities of the seaweed are found in the Sargasso Sea.
    A   B   C   D

20. Giant tortoises live to great ages, and specimens have been known
    A   B
to live from 100 and 150 years.
  C   D

21. Fermentation, the breaking down of simple sugars, produces either
    ____A____
    lactic acid or ethyl alcoholic and carbon dioxide.
    ___B___   _C_   ____D____

22. Most pines grow rapidly and form straight, tall trunks that are ideally for
    __A__   ___B___   _C_   __D__
    lumber.

23. By measuring the color of a star, astronomers can tell how hot is it.
       ____A____ _B_   _C_ _D_

24. Many fruits contain large amounts of vitamin C, as well as sugar, which
    _A_   _____B_____   ___C___
    provide energy.
    ___D___

25. Valuable pearls come from some species of oysters and another mollusks
    ___A___   ____B____
    that live in tropical seas.
    _C_   ___D___

26. Freud's ideas have had a great influence on the study of personality, but
        ___A___   ___B___   _C_
    they are highly controversy.
             _____D_____

27. The Dodge brothers began doing their own automobiles in 1914, and
                              __A__
    produced one of the first American automobiles with an all-steel body.
    _____B_____   _____C_____   ____D____

28. Children's ears are able to detect a wide variety of pitches than adults.
    ___A___   ___B___   _C_   __D__

29. *Euglena* is a single-celled organism that has characteristic of both plants
                  ____A____   _____B_____ _C_ _D_
    and animals.

30. Morse code was an important way to send messages before the tele-
                  _A_   ___B___   ___C___
    phone and radio are invented.
                      __D__

31. Many plains, such the Great Plains in the United States, have few trees
                 __A__   ___B__
    because of dry or cold climates.
    ____C____   ____D____

32. Much psychologists do not associate themselves with a particular school
    _A_   ___B___   _C_   ___D___
    or theory.

33. Prussic acid is one of the most poisonous substances known, neither as
    　　　　　　　　　　　　　　A　　　　　B　　　　C　　　D
    a liquid or a gas.

34. Compact discs, which appeared on the market in the early 1980s,
    　　　　　　　　　A
    produce sound of better quality than those of standard phonograph
    　　B　　　　　　　　　　　　　　　C　　　　　　　　　D
    records.

35. The Pony Express began at a time when not railway went farther west
    　　　　　　　　　　　　　　　　　　A　　B　　　　　　　　C
    than the Mississippi and Missouri rivers.
    　D

36. The Homestead Act of 1862 granted 160 acres of land to any settler
    　　　　　　　　　　　　　　　　　　　　　　　　　　　　　　　A
    which would spend five years on the land.
    　B　　C　　　　　　　　D

37. Dust storms occur however wind erosion is strong and loose material is
    　　　　　　　　　A　　　　　　　　　　B　　　　　　C　　D
    exposed.

38. Pewter ranks as one of the oldest known alloys and may have been used
    　　　A　　　　　　　　　　　B　　　　　　　　　　　C
    as early as 1500 B.C. ago.
    　　　　　　　　　　　D

39. Warm and moisture help microbes grow and thus assist the decay
    　　A　　　　　　　　　　　　　B　　　　C　　　　　　D
    process.

40. Parrots are noisy, sociable birds that live mainly chiefly in forested areas
    　　A　　　　　　　B　　　　　　　　　　C
    in lowlands and mountains.
    　D

PRACTICE TEST 5

Directions

Items in the first part of this section are incomplete sentences. Under each of these sentences, there are four words or phrases. You will choose the *one* word or phrase—(A), (B), (C), or (D)—that best completes the sentence.

EXAMPLE I

Reflexes _____ very valuable in protecting the body against harm.

    (A) that are
    (B) being
    (C) are
    (D) are being

The sentence should read, "Reflexes are very valuable in protecting the body against harm." You should therefore choose (C).

EXAMPLE II

Seismographs are used to locate oil, to determine ocean depth, and _____ and measure earthquakes.

    (A) detect
    (B) to detect
    (C) be detecting
    (D) are detecting

The sentence should read, "Seismographs are used to locate oil, to determine ocean depth, and to detect and measure earthquakes." You should therefore choose (B).

1. The behavior of many volcanoes _____ very difficult to predict, especially the more explosive types.
   - (A) are
   - (B) is
   - (C) that
   - (D) being

2. _____ more than 2,000 minerals are known, nearly all rocks are formed from seven mineral groups.
   - (A) Although
   - (B) However
   - (C) Despite
   - (D) Since

3. Alexander Graham Bell worked with deaf students before _____ the first telephone in 1876.
   - (A) designed
   - (B) was designed
   - (C) to design
   - (D) designing

4. An enzyme works by coming in contact with a particular substance, _____ with it, and changing it.
   - (A) combines
   - (B) combining
   - (C) it combines
   - (D) to combine

5. Foods of animal origin generally supply greater amounts of iron to the diet than _____.
   - (A) are foods of plant origin
   - (B) foods of plant origins
   - (C) do foods of plant origin
   - (D) plant origin foods

6. _____ energy for growth or repair, a plant must carry out photosynthesis.
   - (A) To obtain
   - (B) It obtains
   - (C) It is obtaining
   - (D) Obtaining

7. Nicotine, _____ found in tobacco, is named after the French diplomat Jean Nicot.
   - (A) it is a chemical compound
   - (B) is a chemical compound
   - (C) a chemical compound
   - (D) chemical compound is

8. _____ the world's most successful artificial language.
   - (A) As Esperanto is
   - (B) That Esperanto
   - (C) It is Esperanto
   - (D) Esperanto is

9. _____ food we eat lacks minerals, then the body can use the stores from its bones for more urgent needs.
   - (A) As the
   - (B) If the
   - (C) The
   - (D) Since

10. _____ an organism to become a fossil.
    - (A) Rarely
    - (B) It is rare
    - (C) Rare is
    - (D) It is rare for

11. Among sea horses, _____ carries and hatches the eggs in a special breeding pouch.
    - (A) it is the male which
    - (B) the male it
    - (C) it is the male
    - (D) the male who

12. _____ will be increasingly used as a source of petrochemicals when oil begins to run out.

(A) No matter coal
(B) No doubt coal
(C) If coal
(D) That coal

13. Scientists have discovered that the jellylike material in cells _____ proteins and other substances.

(A) is actually a complex mixture
(B) it is actually a complex mixture
(C) actually is a complex mixture of
(D) that actually are a complex mixture of

14. The discovery that electricity could produce magnetism _____ in 1820 by the Danish physicist, Hans Christian Oersted.

(A) by accident
(B) was an accident
(C) was made by accident
(D) by accident was

15. Digital systems work first by changing quantity and then _____ into strips of numbers.

(A) convert the measurements
(B) the measurements convert
(C) to convert the measurements
(D) converting the measurements

PRACTICE TEST 5

> **Directions**
>
> The rest of the items in this section consist of sentences in which four words or phrases have been underlined. You must identify the *one* underlined expression—(A), (B), (C), or (D)—that must be changed in order to correct the sentence.

EXAMPLE I

Navajo Indians are far more numerous today as they were in the past.
    A   B   C   D

The sentence should read, "Navajo Indians are far more numerous today than they were in the past." You should therefore choose answer (C).

Though it is one of the rarest metals, gold was one of the first to be
  A   B   C
discover.
  D

The sentence should read, "Though it is one of the rarest metals, gold was one of the first to be discovered." You should therefore choose answer (D).

16. National forests including land for animal grazing, as well as wilderness
                    A   B   C
areas with scenic mountains and lakes.
              D

17. The Pony Express from 1860 to 1861 became one of the most colorful
                                          A   B
episodes in American post history.
   C   D

18. Contact lenses made of acrylic are more transparent and least fragile
                                             A   B
than lenses made of glass.
 C   D

19. There is no oxygen in space to support the combustion of fuels as is
          A   B   C
there in the air on Earth.
     D

20. As early as 4000 B.C., people used irons from meteorites to make
                                  A   B
ornaments, weapons, tools and utensils.
    C   D

21. The pioneers <u>raised</u> corn as <u>their</u> chief crop because <u>they</u> kept well in
          A   B   C
    any season and <u>could be</u> used in many ways.
                        D

22. A coral reef consists <u>in millions</u> of tiny coral polyps which are <u>a form of</u>
                               A   B
    small <u>animal</u> <u>related to</u> anemones and jellyfishes.
              C   D

23. In <u>an</u> ordinary <u>optical</u> microscope, <u>a</u> electric bulb or sunlight is used as
          A   B   C
    <u>light</u> for the stage.
       D

24. Eleanor Roosevelt had <u>long a</u> career of public service as a <u>champion</u> of
                              A   B
    <u>human</u> rights, a writer, and a <u>delegate</u> to the United Nations.
        C   D

25. Psychologists use <u>standardized</u> tests to help <u>measure</u> abilities, aptitudes,
                           A   B
    <u>interesting</u>, and <u>personality</u> traits.
         C   D

26. Meriwether Lewis and William Clark <u>were commissioned</u> <u>by</u> the U.S.
                                                A   B
    government to map the <u>lands</u> between St. Louis <u>to</u> the Pacific.
                               C   D

27. <u>As</u> a pure white sugar, dextrose <u>used</u> mainly <u>in</u> candy, baked goods, and
      A   B   C
    <u>canned</u> goods.
        D

28. Paul Dunbar wrote poetry in <u>standard</u> English about <u>tradition</u> poetic
                                     A   B
    subjects and about <u>the</u> <u>heroes</u> of black Americans.
                           C   D

29. It is estimated that <u>at least</u> a <u>million</u> meteors <u>have hit</u> the Earth's land
                              A   B   C
    surface, which is only 25 <u>percentage</u> of the planet.
                                     D

30. The pituitary gland is a small endocrine gland <u>at</u> the base of the brain
                                                        A
    that releases <u>many</u>, hormones and <u>regulates</u> <u>another</u> endocrine glands.
                      B   C   D

31. A persimmon tastes <u>best</u> when it is <u>such</u> ripe that it looks <u>wrinkled</u> and
                           A   B   C
    <u>almost</u> spoiled.
         D

32. American pioneers <u>did</u> water systems from logs with holes <u>bored</u>
                                   A   B
through <u>their</u> <u>centers</u>.
          C   D

33. Polls <u>following</u> <u>scientific</u> procedures began in 1935 with the <u>experiment</u>
            A   B   C
nationwide <u>surveys</u> of George Gallup and Elm Roper.
                D

34. In America, the Indians used crude oil for <u>fuel</u> and medicine <u>hundreds</u> of
                                                   A   B
years <u>before</u> the first white settlers <u>arrive</u>.
       C   D

35. When radio programs <u>became</u> popular, <u>approximately</u> around 1925,
        A   B   C
many people stopped <u>attending</u> movies.
                     D

36. Musical comedies, <u>as</u> an American form of <u>entertainment</u>, often take <u>its</u>
                         A   B   C
subjects from America's present <u>or</u> past.
                                   D

37. Of all seashore plants, seaweeds are <u>best</u> able to tolerate long periods
    A   B
out of water, followed <u>by</u> long periods <u>covering</u> by water.
                        C   D

38. The fruit of the plantain looks <u>much</u> like a banana, <u>and</u> it is not so sweet
                                     A   B
or so <u>pleasing</u> in <u>flavor</u>.
       C   D

39. The viceroy butterfly, an insect <u>that</u> birds like to eat, has a color pattern
                                   A
similar <u>to</u> that <u>of</u> the monarch butterfly, <u>whom</u> birds do not like to eat.
        B   C   D

40. Behavior therapy uses rewards and <u>punishments</u> to encourage patients
                                           A
to act <u>in</u> a <u>way</u> healthier.
 B   C   D

ANSWER KEY

CHAPTER 1
Exercise 1
1. information
2. women's
3. one-fourth
4. language, logic
5. art, music
6. pounds
7. pain
8. million nerve

Exercise 2
1. F
2. T
3. F
4. T
5. F
6. F

Exercise 3
1. Intelligence is the ability to use thought and knowledge to understand things and solve problems.
2. Hormones help adjust the mixture of sugar, salt, and water in your body.
3. Psychology, the study of the mind and how it works, comes from a Greek word meaning life or soul.
4. Brain cells use up a lot of energy, so they need a constant supply of oxygen.
5. Each hemisphere of the brain receives information about the opposite side of the visual field.
6. Although millions of brain neurons are active at any one time, they do not use much electric power.
7. Light entering the eye forms an image on 130 million tiny light cells.
8. Most animals are not able to rely on learning and memory.

Exercise 4
1. People's brains weigh more now than they did 100 years ago.
2. Nerve impulses travel at speeds of up to 488 feet per second.
3. The brain contains between 10 trillion and 100 trillion neurons.
4. Each neuron is linked by synapses to thousands of other neurons.
5. Nerve endings below the skin's surface pick up sensations of cold, heat, and touch.
6. There are three to four million pain receptors in the skin.
7. A three-year-old child's brain is two-thirds the size it will finally be.
8. The brain uses twenty-five percent of the blood's oxygen.

Exercise ON NOUNS
1. D
2. A
3. C
4. A
5. B
6. A.
7. A
8. D
9. A
10. C
11. D
12. D

CHAPTER 2
Exercise 1
1. They live in Antarctica.
2. She produces one egg.
3. He uses a special fold of skin.
4. They stand together to protect themselves from the cold.
5. They put their eggs on their feet.
6. She goes to find food.
7. She returns after two months.
8. He returns to the sea.

Exercise 2
1. T
2. T
3. F
4. F
5. F
6. F
7. T
8. F

Exercise 3
1. she
2. He
3. She
4. I
5. He
6. they

Exercise 4
1. He helps her take care of the baby penguin.
2. Correct
3. Correct
4. It is not easy for them to survive under such conditions.
5. It is harder for him than for her.
6. Correct

Exercise 5
1. her
2. his
3. their
4. its
5. their
6. her

Exercise 6
1. his
2. theirs
3. theirs
4. ours
5. hers
6. mine

Exercise 7
1. themselves
2. itself
3. herself
4. itself/himself
5. himself
6. ourselves

Exercise 8
1. There are eighteen different kinds of penguins that live south of the equator.
2. The biologist who went to the south pole is studying emperor penguins.
3. The Emperor penguins survive winds that blow at speeds of up to ninety-five miles an hour in winter.
4. Correct
5. The emperor penguins, which are the largest among penguins, do not make nests.
6. The United States has sent researchers to Antarctica who are making experiments to measure the energy expended by emperor penguins.

Exercise ON PRONOUNS
1. B
2. C
3. D
4. D
5. D
6. A
7. A
8. B
9. D
10. C
11. D
12. A

CHAPTER 3
Exercise 1
1. At the Boston slave market, <u>Phyllis</u> (was purchased) by John Wheatley.
2. In a few years, <u>Phyllis</u> (had learned) geography, history, and Latin.
3. <u>Her mistress, Mrs. Wheatley,</u> (was impressed) by the child's aptitude.
4. At the age of thirteen, <u>she</u> (wrote) her first poem.
5. In 1773 <u>her first book of poems</u> (was published.)
6. With the London publication of her book, <u>her fame</u> (spread) on both sides of the Atlantic.

Exercise 2
1. C
2. NC
3. C
4. NC
5. C
6. C

Exercise 3
1. C
2. B
3. A
4. B
5. C
6. D

Exercise 4
1. B
2. A
3. D
4. A
5. C

ANSWER KEY

Exercise ON PARTS OF A SENTENCE
1. A
2. C
3. B
4. D
5. A
6. B
7. D
8. D
9. B
10. D
11. C
12. A

CHAPTER 4
Exercise 1
1. comes
2. abolished
3. discovered
4. proposed
5. has been held
6. were
7. were admitted

Exercise 2
1. The Olympics took place every four years from 776 B.C. to 394 A.D.
2. Correct
3. From 1896 to the present, the Olympic Games have been held every four years.
4. Correct
5. With this international competition Pierre de Corubertin wanted to encourage both sport and world peace.
6. In 1916, 1940, and 1944 the Olympic Games did not take place.

Exercise 3
1. A
2. B
3. C
4. D
5. A
6. B
7. B
8. D

Exercise 4
1. was held
2. was built
3. was flown
4. was led
5. were cancelled
6. were shown

Exercise 5
1. A
2. B
3. A
4. B
5. B
6. A

Exercise ON VERBS
1. B
2. A
3. C
4. D
5. A
6. B
7. B
8. C
9. B
10. B
11. C
12. C

CHAPTER 5
Exercise 1
1. on
2. by
3. In, of
4. by
5. with
6. from, on

Exercise 2
1. A potato famine occurred in Ireland in the 1840s. Due to the famine 1.5 million people died.
2. A flood occurred in Johnstown, Pennsylvania, U.S., in May 1889. Due to the flood 2,200 people died.
3. An earthquake occurred in Tangshan, China, on July 28, 1976. Due to the earthquake 242,000 people died.
4. A tidal wave occurred in Bangladesh in 1970. Due to the tidal wave 200,000 people died.
5. A tornado occurred in Ohio, U.S., on April 3, 1974. Due to the tornado 315 people died.
6. A fire occurred in Yellowstone Park, U.S., in 1980. Due to the fire 1.3 million acres burned.

Exercise 3
1. to
2. from
3. in
4. to
5. by
6. on
7. to
8. on

Exercise 4
1. to
2. for
3. of
4. for
5. from
6. to
7. on
8. at

Exercise 5
1. of
2. for
3. of
4. of
5. of
6. on
7. of
8. of

Exercise 6
1. to
2. to
3. of
4. of
5. of
6. of
7. of
8. to

Exercise 7
1. in
2. at, on
3. on
4. In, in
5. in
6. in, in
7. of
8. in, in
9. from, to
10. from, to

Exercise 8
1. on
2. At
3. In
4. in
5. on
6. on
7. In
8. by

Exercise ON PREPOSITIONS
1. D
2. A
3. C
4. C
5. B
6. D
7. B
8. B
9. D
10. A
11. A
12. B

CHAPTER 6

Exercise 1
1. Japan
2. Greenland
3. Australia
4. Great Britain
5. Iceland
6. Surtsey

Exercise 2
1. Arctic
2. New Guinea, Pacific
3. Borneo, the third, the Pacific
4. Madagascar, the fourth, the Indian
5. Baffin Island, the Arctic
6. Sumatra, the fifth, the Pacific

Exercise 3
1. C
2. NC, a big island
3. C
4. C
5. an uninhabited island
6. C
7. C
8. C
9. animals

Exercise 4
1. the, ø, the
2. The,
3. ø, ø, a
4. The, ø, a
5. The, ø, a, ø
6. the, the, ø
7. the, the, ø
8. the, the, ø
9. ø, a, the
10. The, the, the

ANSWER KEY

Exercise ON ARTICLES
1. D
2. B
3. A
4. A
5. D
6. C
7. B
8. B
9. D
10. B
11. A
12. D

CHAPTER 7
Exercise 1
1. that
2. that
3. how
4. that/how
5. that
6. that

Exercise 2
1. A
2. B
3. A
4. B
5. B

Exercise 3
1. NC
2. C
3. C
4. NC
5. NC
6. C

Exercise 4
1. C
2. A
3. A
4. B
5. C
6. D

Exercise ON NOUN CLAUSES
1. A
2. B
3. C
4. D
5. A
6. B
7. A
8. D
9. A
10. B
11. B
12. C

CHAPTER EIGHT
Exercise 1
1. which
2. whose
3. who
4. which
5. which
6. which

Exercise 2
1. which
2. which
3. which
4. which
5. which
6. who

Exercise 3
1. Sacagewea. who was a Shoshoni Indian, guided Lewis and Clark to the Columbia River.
2. The giant redwood trees that grow in California, are named after Sequoyah, who created an alphabet for the Indian people.
3. Sequoyah became a teacher and moved to Oklahoma where he continued to teach the alphabet.
4. The Shoshoni were a group of Indians who lived in the western plains of Wyoming, Utah, Nevada, and Idaho.
5. Each group of Shoshoni was known to the others by the type of food that was plentiful in its particular region.
6. The Mossi people of West Africa use talking drums as a means of preserving their history, which has been handed down by generations.

Exercise 4
2, 3, 5, 6,

Exercise 5
1. Sequoyah, the son of an Indian mother and a European father, was born in Tennessee.
2. Sequoyah, first a hunter, became a trader after a hunting accident.
3. Correct
4. Correct
5. His alphabet consisting of eighty-five sounds was an important invention for his people.
6. Correct
7. Correct

Exercise ON ADJECTIVE CLAUSES
1. A
2. B
3. C
4. D
5. A
6. B
7. C
8. D
9. B
10. A
11. C
12. D

Exercise ON ADVERB CLAUSES
1. B
2. B
3. B
4. D
5. C
6. B
7. B
8. D
9. C
10. D
11. B
12. A

CHAPTER NINE
Exercise 1
1. before
2. when
3. when
4. because
5. when
6. although

Exercise 2
1. because
2. as
3. where
4. after
5. whereas
6. before

Exercise 3
1. <u>Although millions of meteors hit the earth's atmosphere</u>, few of them are noticed.
2. A meteor leaves a bright trail <u>as it streaks across the night sky</u>.
3. Many meteorite falls are not noticed <u>because they hit the earth in remote uninhabited areas</u>.
4. The rate of the sun's radiation is so great <u>that about 3 million tons of matter is converted into energy every second</u>.
5. In ancient times, farmers planted crops <u>when they saw a planet in the right part of the sky</u>.
6. <u>Even though a planet moves among the stars</u>, it returns to the same part of the sky at the same time each year.

Exercise 4
1. A
2. B
3. C
4. D
5. B
6. B

CHAPTER TEN
Exercise 1
1. in, in
2. in, in, of
3. by
4. from, in, in
5. in, by
6. in

Exercise 2
1. Richard Long leaves his mark by making changes in the landscape.
2. Richard Long brings back found objects from his walks.
3. Richard Long uses the objects in sculptures that are shown in art galleries.
4. Land art involves the artist going into nature, usually in a remote area.
5. The only record that remains of land art is photographic, sometimes combined with maps.

Exercise 3
1. Artists have painted nature for centuries.
      S   V   O   PP
2. Richard Long recorded his work
          S   V   O
   in different ways.
       PP
3. Most murals are painted
       S   V
   in a naturalistic style.
       PP
4. The role of art in western culture
          S
   has changed in the last hundred years.
       V   PP
5. Futurism emerged in northern Italy
      S   V   PP
   before the First World War.
       PP
6. Some contemporary artists have rejected
         S   V
   art galleries for political reasons.
     O   PP

ANSWER KEY

Exercise 4
1. The invention of photography <u>in the 1820s</u> encouraged artists to attempt even greater realism <u>in their paintings</u>.
2. As the 19th century wore on, some artists began to question the need for art to refer <u>to the outside world</u>.
3. By the <u>19th century</u>, art dealers had begun to sell uncommissioned art <u>to a wider public</u>.
4. Monet was more concerned <u>with expressing an almost mystical sense of communion with nature</u> than <u>with working spontaneously</u>.
5. <u>With the Industrial Revolution</u> the landscape began to change more and more, and artists began to look into its negative and positive aspects.
6. Land are involves the artist going out <u>into nature, usually in a remote area</u>, and making his or her mark <u>on it</u>.

Exercise 5
1. A
2. B
3. C
4. D
5. A
6. B
7. B
8. D

Exercise ON PREPOSITIONAL PHRASES
1. B
2. A
3. C
4. D
5. A
6. B
7. C
8. D
9. A
10. B
11. C
12. D

CHAPTER ELEVEN
Exercise 1
1. lesser
2. smallest, highest
3. larger
4. richer
5. brilliant
6. greatest

Exercise 2
1. biggest
2. smaller
3. bigger
4. big
5. big
6. smallest

Exercise 3
1. highest
2. importantest
3. more older
4. sound (as omitted)
5. low
6. short
7. more
8. the

Exercise ON COMPARATIVES AND SUPERLATIVES
1. A
2. B
3. C
4. D
5. B
6. A
7. C
8. C
9. B
10. B
11. B
12. C

CHAPTER TWELVE
Exercise 1
1. and
2. and
3. and
4. but
5. and
6. and

Exercise 2
1. Soya is not only used in many food processes but also in many industrial processes.
2. Soya has been used in the manufacture of paints both for industrial and domestic use.
3. Glycerine is not only used in glues but also in the manufacture of explosives.
4. Soya is used in the manufacture of food both for human consumption and animal consumption.
5. American farmers have been encouraged to grow more soya not only because the export market has expanded but also because the demand at home has increased.
6. The ancient Chinese used the soya bean for both food and medicine.

Exercise 3
1. B
2. A
3. C
4. D
5. A
6. B
7. A
8. B

Exercise ON CONJUNCTIONS
1. A
2. C
3. D
4. C
5. B
6. B
7. B
8. C
9. D
10. B
11. D
12. D

CHAPTER THIRTEEN
Exercise 1
1. fresh vegetables, fruit
2. gums bled, their skin became rough, their wounds did not heal, their muscles wasted away.
3. heat, storage, exposure to air
4. the elderly, alcoholics, the chronically ill
5. speeds would healing, helps prevent gum disease, helps protect us from pollutants such as cigarette smoke.
6. increases life span.

Exercise 2
For
1. Lowers cholesterol and fights heart disease.
2. Correct
3. Correct
4. Fights diabetes.
5. Fights gum disease.
6. Strengthens immunity against colds.

Against
1. Wastes money because the body excretes excess vitamin C.
2. Causes kidney stones in some people.
3. Causes diarrhea and stomach cramps in some people.
4. Correct

Exercise 3
1. Vitamin E <u>protects against heart disease</u>, <u>prevents cancer</u>, and <u>fights skin problems</u>. (V)
2. The mineral fluoride is found naturally in <u>soils</u>, <u>water</u>, <u>plants</u>, and <u>animal tissue</u>. (N)
3. The tomato plant needs a <u>long growing</u> season and <u>light</u>, <u>rich</u>, <u>well-drained</u> soil. (ADJ)
4. Vitamin E is being employed <u>slowly</u> but <u>steadily</u> in medicine in an expanding range of ailments. (ADV)
5. Studies have shown that vitamin C can reduce <u>the severity and lengths</u> of colds, but not <u>the number of colds a person gets</u>. (N)
6. If you do not have enough iron, you can suffer from anemia, which makes you <u>pale</u>, <u>tired</u>, and <u>weak</u>. (ADJ)

Exercise 4
1. Iron-deficiency anemia has been implicated in <u>emotion</u>, social, and learning difficulties in infants, adolescents, and adults.
2. All "B" vitamins are needed for healthy appetite, energy production in cells, and healthy <u>nervous</u> and skin.
3. Some <u>vitamins may</u> cause toxic, <u>allergy</u> reactions in some people.
4. Symptoms of a mild case of vitamin C deficiency may be weakness, <u>irritable</u>, loss of weight, and apathy.
5. Claims that vitamin C will prevent, <u>relief</u>, or cure colds and winter illnesses are unwarranted according to Hodges.
6. Magnesium deficiency is characterized by loss of appetite, nausea, <u>confusing</u>, loss of coordination, and tremors.

Exercise 5
1. Some people take vitamin E to relieve muscular cramps, to extend life span, and fight skin problems.
2. The Nobel Laureate Dr. Linus Pauling persistently claimed that vitamin C is effective in preventing and alleviating colds and treating cancer.
3. Many food processes such as drying, flavoring, canning, and tenderizing may add salt.
4. It is important to select foods that are in their best state, store them properly, and prepare them to ensure the maximum retention of vitamin C.
5. Avoiding the purchase of foods with salt content while marketing or eating out is helpful.
6. The major function of vitamin D is to ensure an adequate supply of calcium and phosphorus in the bones, to prevent rickets in children, and maintain good levels of calcium and phosphorus in the blood.

Exercise 6
1. Very large intakes of any of the essential nutrients may result in both undesirable toxic symptoms and serious side effects.
2. Minerals in the cell influence not only the vital processes of oxidation but also secretion and growth.
3. Many people feel that both frozen and canned fruits and vegetables are inferior to fresh produce.
4. Canned food can neither be kept for unlimited lengths of time nor be kept at any temperature.
5. Fruit grown either sheltered from sunlight or grown in a season of many rainy days will not have much vitamin C.
6. Good peaches should be neither too hard, nor too soft.

Exercise ON PARALLEL STRUCTURE
1. D
2. D
3. C
4. D
5. D
6. C
7. A
8. B
9. C
10. D
11. B
12. C

CHAPTER FOURTEEN
Exercise 1
1. It is relatively easy for computers to speak.
2. Until recently it was thought computers would have to be programmed to the accent and speech habits of the user.
3. It is claimed that the IBM Tangora system can recognize a spoken vocabulary of 20,000 words.
4. Statistical probability is necessary for computers to interpret not only speech but visual data as well.
5. Up to now computers have not been programmed to react to a range of spoken commands.
6. The machine can calculate the probability of one particular word following another.

Exercise 2
1. Not until
2. Never
3. Not only
4. Not until
5. Only
6. Nor

Exercise 3
1. Should you make an error, it can be corrected easily.
2. On a magnetic disc information is stored.
3. Had he been more careful, we would not have lost all that data.
4. Not only does the computer store information, but also distributes it.
5. No sooner were personal computers invented than typewriters began to be replaced.
6. Only recently has the impact of the computer been strongly felt.

Exercise 4
1. D
2. A
3. B
4. B
5. D
6. B

Exercise ON INVERSION
1. C
2. C
3. A
4. D
5. B
6. C
7. A
8. C
9. B
10. D
11. A
12. B

CHAPTER FIFTEEN
Exercise 1
1. inventor/scientist
2. printer
3. politician
4. dangerous
5. thick, metal
6. use

Exercise 2
1. F
2. F
3. T
4. T
5. T
6. T

Exercise 3
1. politician
2. inventor
3. science
4. printer
5. physicist
6. chemistry

Exercise 4
1. activate
2. thicken
3. sympathize
4. regularize
5. solidify
6. lighten

Exercise 5
1. entertainment
2. freedom
3. discovered
4. sign
5. service
6. developed

Exercise 6
1. successful
2. interested
3. weekly
4. safely
5. smokeless
6. good

Exercise 7
1. ADJ
2. N
3. N
4. N
5. ADJ
6. N/V
7. N
8. N
9. ADV
10. N

Exercise 8
1. ADJ
2. V
3. ADJ
4. ADV
5. N
6. V
7. N
8. ADJ

Exercise ON WORD FORMS
1. B
2. D
3. B
4. A
5. B
6. C
7. D
8. D
9. C
10. A
11. A
12. A

CHAPTER SIXTEEN
Exercise 1
1. Unlike
2. so
3. After
4. almost
5. but
6. and

Exercise 2
1. b
2. a
3. d
4. e
5. c

ANSWER KEY

Exercise 3
1. do, done, made
2. made
3. do
4. made
5. made
6. made

Exercise 4
1. Unlike
2. alike
3. Like
4. like
5. unlike
6. alike

Exercise 5
1. Another
2. other
3. another
4. other
5. other
6. the other

Exercise 6
1. so
2. so
3. too
4. so
5. such
6. too

Exercise 7
1. Much
2. much
3. many
4. little, many
5. Few
6. little

Exercise 8
1. A number
2. Because of
3. not
4. After
5. some
6. most

Exercise 9
1, 2, 3, 6, 7, 8

Exercise ON WORD CHOICE AND REDUNDANCY
1. C
2. C
3. B
4. C
5. D
6. B
7. B
8. B
9. C
10. A
11. C
12. A

PRACTICE TEST 1
1. D
2. B
3. A
4. A
5. B
6. C
7. D
8. A
9. B
10. D
11. B
12. C
13. D
14. A
15. B
16. B
17. A
18. D
19. C
20. A
21. B
22. D
23. C
24. D
25. A
26. B
27. A
28. C
29. D
30. B
31. C
32. C
33. B
34. C
35. C
36. A
37. C
38. D
39. A
40. B

PRACTICE TEST 2

1. B
2. A
3. C
4. B
5. D
6. C
7. A
8. B
9. C
10. D
11. A
12. B
13. A
14. C
15. D
16. D
17. D
18. D
19. C
20. D
21. B
22. B
23. B
24. C
25. D
26. D
27. B
28. C
29. A
30. D
31. C
32. D
33. C
34. B
35. C
36. C
37. C
38. D
39. C
40. B

PRACTICE TEST 3

1. A
2. C
3. B
4. D
5. A
6. B
7. D
8. A
9. C
10. B
11. A
12. C
13. D
14. A
15. D
16. C
17. C
18. D
19. D
20. A
21. B
22. C
23. B
24. D
25. B
26. D
27. A
28. C
29. D
30. D
31. B
32. C
33. C
34. C
35. B
36. A
37. D
38. D
39. D
40. D

ANSWER KEY

PRACTICE TEST 4
1. A
2. B
3. D
4. C
5. D
6. B
7. C
8. A
9. C
10. B
11. D
12. A
13. B
14. C
15. D
16. D
17. B
18. A
19. C
20. D
21. D
22. D
23. D
24. D
25. B
26. D
27. A
28. C
29. B
30. D
31. A
32. A
33. D
34. C
35. B
36. B
37. A
38. D
39. A
40. C

PRACTICE TEST 5
1. B
2. A
3. D
4. B
5. C
6. A
7. C
8. D
9. B
10. D
11. A
12. B
13. C
14. C
15. D
16. A
17. D
18. B
19. C
20. A
21. C
22. A
23. C
24. A
25. C
26. D
27. B
28. B
29. D
30. D
31. B
32. A
33. C
34. D
35. C
36. C
37. D
38. B
39. D
40. D

NOTES

Virtually anything is possible @ petersons.com

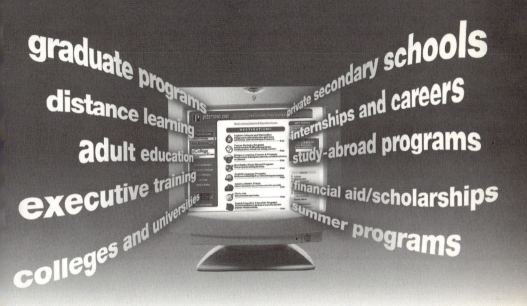

graduate programs
distance learning
adult education
executive training
colleges and universities
private secondary schools
internships and careers
study-abroad programs
financial aid/scholarships
summer programs

Peterson's quality with every click!

Whether you're a high school student headed for college or a busy professional interested in distance learning, you'll find all of the tools you need, literally at your fingertips!

Petersons.com is your ultimate online adviser, connecting you with "virtually any" educational or career need.

Count on us to show you how to:

Apply to more than 1,200 colleges online

Finance the education of your dreams

Find a summer camp for your child

Make important career choices

Earn a degree online

Search executive education programs

Visit us today at **petersons.com**
AOL Keyword: Petersons

Peterson's unplugged

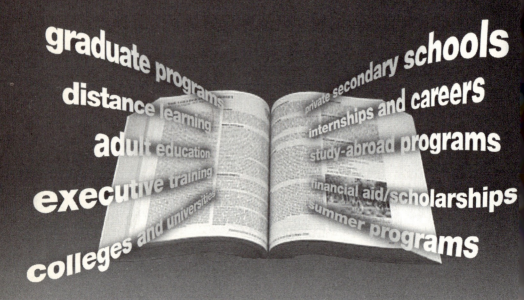

Peterson's quality on every page!

For more than three decades, we've offered a complete selection of books to guide you in all of your educational endeavors. You can find our vast collection of titles at your local bookstore or online at **petersons.com**.

High school student headed for college?

Busy professional interested in distance learning?

Parent searching for the perfect private school or summer camp?

Human resource manager looking for executive education programs?

AOL Keyword: Petersons
Phone: 800-338-3282